A

Archaeology and History

Archaeology and History

A plea for reconciliation

D. P. Dymond

THAMES AND HUDSON · LONDON

First published 1974

© *Thames and Hudson Ltd 1974*

All Rights Reserved. No part of this publication
may be reproduced or transmitted in any form
or by any means, electronic or mechanical, including
photocopy, recording or any information storage
and retrieval system, without permission in writing,
from the publisher.

Printed and bound in Singapore by Tien Wah Press, Singapore.

ISBN 0 500 05013

Contents

Part II—Examples of Co-ordination

Foreword

Having been trained as an historian, and then by the accidents of the employment market found myself a professional archaeologist, I have long been troubled by what has seemed to be the unsatisfactory relationship between the worlds of archaeology and history. Of recent years the demands of extra-mural teaching have confirmed my misgivings: non-specialist audiences rightly want their questions answered by means of *all* relevant evidence, and are not great respecters of ill-defined academic boundaries. This book has therefore been written in the belief that there needs to be a vast improvement in the relations between the two disciplines, and if it contributes in some small way to better understanding, I will account it successful. Part I is a discussion of the nature and definition of archaeological and historical evidence, the methods and principles used by both sides, and the inevitable overlapping which occurs. Part II briefly reviews examples of co-ordination, both past and present. It ends with an appeal for 'total archaeology' which is surely the most far-reaching and curative of all kinds of co-ordination, because it encourages the widest-possible definition of archaeology and necessitates the use of a great range of documents. Most of the examples used throughout Parts I and II are British, but it is hoped nevertheless that the basic theme and ideas are of wider application.

I am indebted to many people for help and advice. Dr Glyn Daniel first persuaded me to undertake the task and has given me encouragement throughout. Valuable criticisms have been received from A. R. Allan, Professor W. G. Hoskins, Mrs Dorothy Owen, Norman Scarfe, C. C. Taylor, Dr D. Trump and Dr R. Virgoe. I would like to record my particular gratitude

to two friends, D. J. Bonney and D. Holland, with whom I
have had many helpful discussions over the years on the common ground between history and archaeology. The typing of
several drafts of the book was kindly undertaken by Mrs Nancy
Tripp. Finally, I am happy to thank my father for help with
the index, and my wife and three children for their support and
tolerance throughout the period when the book was taking shape.

D.D.

Part I: *Archaeology and History*

1 Historical and archaeological evidence

Some explanation of the title I have given to this book is perhaps called for. At first glance, the two disciplines of archaeology and history seem distinct enough. The two subjects are
normally taught and examined separately – in fact the academic
training of the two professions is quite specialized, and contacts
between them are not commonplace. Why therefore consider
the two together?

Although they show considerable differences in approach,
raw materials and methods, both professions deal with human
life in the past; this itself is enough to relate them closely. But
increasingly they are actually working on the same periods
and human groups. Although archaeologists have been traditionally concerned with prehistory, that immense span of time
for which no written records survive – without archaeology
there could be no prehistory – they are now working on later
periods, which have hitherto been the exclusive domain of the
historian: this is because there are many submerged aspects of
those periods which are not revealed, or only partially revealed,
by documents. Furthermore, if documentary and physical
evidence both exist for a certain subject, then surely a co-
ordinated study must be nearer the goal of complete truth than
a simple documentary or archaeological treatment. If such a
synthesis is to be achieved, then obviously there must be mutual
understanding and an acknowledgement of the things in common, as well as the undoubted differences.

In view of the increasing chronological overlap and the
attempt by a few scholars to synthesize the two kinds of evidence,
this would seem an opportune moment to discuss the relationship between archaeology and history. What for example is
archaeological evidence, and what distinguishes it from historical
evidence? What are the principles on which archaeologists
and historians analyze their raw-material? Is the ultimate

purpose of the archaeologist any different from that of the
historian? Can different kinds of historical evidence be satisfactorily integrated? Basic to the consideration of these and
other problems is the definition of our terms.

In general usage, the word *history* has, and has had, several
meanings which need to be carefully unravelled. With its
European equivalents, it is based on a Greek word meaning
'knowledge' or 'inquiry'. Perhaps the English phrase which
comes closest to the Greek is *Natural History*, which is an
inquiry into the world of plants and animals. But because any
form of knowledge or inquiry is bound to take notice of the
element of time, and particularly of time past, history became
increasingly associated with the past, and the changes which
time has brought. Darwin's theory of evolution is a classic
demonstration of this in the study of the natural order. In fact
several scientific specializations like geology, palaeontology
and astronomy are as concerned with time as is the orthodox
historian in the field of purely human affairs.

Gradually two broad meanings of the word *history* emerged.
The first was a relation of events, a narrative or story – whether
true or imaginary. When in the 18th century the English novel-
ist Henry Fielding wrote his characterful 'histories' (of Tom
Jones, Jonathan Wild, Joseph Andrews, etc.) he was using
the word as simply a story, and this still remains of course one
meaning of the modern French *histoire*. The second, narrower
meaning is the narrative or record of the human past, which
is, professedly at least, true. This covers the constructed account of past events by the historian, and is of course the normal
use of the word in English today. In this sense history obviously
includes the work of both historians and archaeologists, as they
both contribute to the record of human life in the past (regard-
less of the fact that they use different kinds of evidence).

More recently another quite specialized meaning has come
into circulation, though it is rarely found in dictionaries. It
denotes the study of the human past *from documentary sources
alone*. By documents, we mean all written sources, whether
manuscript, printed or inscribed. This is primarily of course
the field of the regular historian, whose job it is to interpret
written or verbal evidence.

This last meaning of the word is used by archaeologists when
they refer to prehistory, proto-history and the like.[1] Here
history means the written records of literate societies, referring

to themselves and sometimes their illiterate neighbours. Before the advent of literacy (or its survival), the human past can only be studied from physical or archaeological traces. By *prehistoric* some archaeologists mean societies which existed before there was documentary evidence anywhere, that is before approximately 3000 BC when written records first appear in the Near East. Others, not so ruthlessly logical, call societies prehistoric which pre-date the *local* arrival of literacy. In spite of this difference of opinion, all are agreed that *history* in this connection means written records. It is of some interest that the coining of the term *prehistoric* in the 19th century (it has now been traced back in its French form to M. Tournal in 1833) seems to have fostered the narrow definition of *history*. In other words, people with largely archaeological interests encouraged, and perhaps even originated, a new definition of the word *history*, because they wished to emphasize the crucial difference between periods that are documented and those that are not.[2]

Finally, there is yet another usage of the word which in one important respect shakes free of the Greek root. Whereas all the definitions so far discussed have involved some kind of personal study, in this final sense *history* is used to describe the actual events of the past. It is, in other words, the past as opposed to our reconstruction of it. Although history in this sense is not recoverable (because we have no means of knowing it save through our sources and their interpretation), the distinction is a vital one which reminds us that the past does have an objective existence, and is an ideal standard of truth to which we aspire.

The word *archaeology* has also had more than one usage. Etymologically it too comes from Greek, and means the study of antiquity. It has been used in a general sense which is indistinguishable from the broad meaning of history, as the study of man's past. For example, Plato in his *Hippias Maior* described archaeology as a science which comprises such things as genealogy, lists of magistrates, and oral traditions. In 1803 a writer in *Archaeologia* was able to say that 'the contents of the Archaiology (sic) of Wales are derived from various collections of old manuscripts,' thus equating it with history in the narrow sense. But increasingly from the 19th century onwards, the word has been used to describe the study of antiquities or ancient *things*. In other words, it is the study of the material evidence of the human past, and involves objects which can be seen, handled, measured and classified.

This analysis underlines a problem which every specialist faces: the imprecision and ambiguity of language. When we use a word we assume a certain meaning and interpretation for it, but this may not be obvious to our readers or listeners. A further complication is that words change their meanings, albeit slowly. So we must be quite clear in our own minds what we intend to convey by certain words and phrases, and be prepared if necessary to define them. As Glyn Daniel has said (in discussing whether archaeology is a science) 'we ourselves have made these terms science, humanities, the arts, the human sciences, and whether a new branch of learning which we as scholars have created, developed and refined, falls within any of these terms depends on how we define them and how we have defined them in the past.'[3]

To return to the two words *archaeology* and *history*, there is still no consistency in our use of them today. While Professor Piggott writes that 'archaeology is in fact a branch of historical study,' Professor Atkinson can say that 'the archaeologist has but little claim to be a kind of historian.'[4] The difference between those statements (and scores of others) depends quite simply on different underlying definitions, which admittedly are not made any clearer by quoting out of context. Sometimes one knows, or can guess, which meaning a writer or speaker has in mind, but on other occasions one needs to devote considerable thought to semantics. Because language is constantly evolving, problems of meaning and definition will always be with us. It is part of the working life of every specialist that he should struggle with words: historians and archaeologists are no worse off than many other groups. However, the confusion is sometimes so great that one is tempted to quote a number as a reference to the meaning intended in a standard dictionary; perhaps Henry Ford ought to have said that 'history (3) is bunk (2)'!

Having accepted that, in the modern sense of the word, archaeology is concerned with material evidence, one should follow the implications further. Archaeological evidence can be any object which has been associated with human life in the past. Normally it consists of 'artifacts', that is products of human workmanship. These can be small and portable, such as a stone axe or a tinder-box, or they can be larger, immovable 'monuments' like a hut-circle, a factory or a field-system. Artifacts and monuments can be commonplace or rare: a simple tool or a work of art; a burial mound or a sophisticated cathedral. In addition, providing they have some clear connection with human life, archaeological evidence can also consist of completely *natural* objects, such as animal bones, pollen grains, caves, layers of soil, and even defined areas of landscape.

That the same things can be evidence for other specialists does not matter; indeed, it is a positive advantage. For example, animal bones found in an archaeological excavation can provide new evidence for zoologists, and pollen grains buried in mud or peat are of immense importance to botanists. Such converging interests are of benefit to all; they enable specialists to exchange information obtained by quite different methods, and underline the essential unity of all knowledge. Today it is noticeable that most natural, physical and social sciences are becoming more and more interested in the dimension of time. Equally, archaeologists are constantly looking for scientific techniques which will enable them to extract more information from material objects. This has always been the case since archaeology was born as a separate discipline in the early 19th century, but now the pace of interchange has speeded up enormously.

It should go without saying that archaeological evidence can be of any period before the present. Although in practice, archaeology has been mainly concerned with prehistory, and has developed and refined its techniques in this field, the past can only be satisfactorily defined by reference to the present. One can therefore quite logically define as old anything which was made before today, or before that moving instant of time which we call the present. So an obsolete petrol pump, a municipal rubbish tip or, indeed, a brand-new car are theoretically archaeological evidence informative of human life, in the same way as burial-mounds and arrowheads. This is a point which has been made many times: O. G. S. Crawford referred to obsolete aircraft as strictly archaeological, while Gordon Childe similarly speculated about the remains of his picnic lunch on Esher Common. We, like our predecessors, are busily creating our own archaeological record. Given time, this may be investigated by future archaeologists who wish to throw light on some aspect of our period which is not revealed by written documents. As a widespread example of the 20th-century archaeological record, one could quote the traces of two world wars which still litter Europe: bunkers, cemeteries, airfields, redeveloped towns and much else.

Although the physical and temporal range of archaeological evidence is clearly enormous, it does not follow that every collector of vintage cars, stamps, beer-mats or antiques is necessarily an archaeologist. If, as is usually the case, his main interest is in the objects themselves, as bits of machinery, or pretty designs, or as rare specimens, he is in fact behaving like the traditional antiquary, who valued his specimens more than the historical information they yielded. Nor need the point be confined to collectors: for example one has the feeling that some industrial archaeologists are really latter-day antiquarians, concerned with technical detail for its own sake rather than in the resultant social and economic history.

Another result of the vast range of archaeological data is that subdivision and specialization are inevitable. Several self-contained subjects have split off in the past, and the process is still going on today. Art-history is a case in point; the study of physical works of art such as paintings and sculpture, clearly involves archaeological evidence and is really a specialist branch of archaeology. It is the special distinction of works of art that, whereas most physical objects were not meant as a form of conscious communication, they were deliberately made to communicate thoughts and feelings, and they are therefore the most highly developed form of physical evidence (see p. 126). Architectural history and numismatics have similarly diverged from the main line of archaeology, and there are other specialities based on periods and localities rather than on types of artifact. In all these, although the techniques involved are far more than simply archaeological – for instance the study of documents and various kinds of scientific analysis are involved – the subject matter is archaeological because it is physical and from the past.

Some people have said that archaeological evidence may not in every case be physical. What about, they ask, the 'ghost' features or impressions of objects which have otherwise disappeared? Did the great boat at Sutton Hoo, when it was first excavated in 1939 and re-excavated in 1967, really exist? Do the cavities at Pompeii which Fiorelli showed were the impressions of human bodies really constitute physical evidence?

Or the small holes in the ground at Ur, from which Sir Leonard
Woolley cast the outlines of a prehistoric harp? The definition
does of course stand, because, although in these cases the
positive object has decayed irretrievably and has changed its
physical character, it is still recognizable as a volume of material
or as a vacuum, and furthermore the negative impression is
itself a physical phenomenon. Exactly the same reasoning can
be applied to other archaeological features such as post-holes
and robber trenches – in all these the 'ghost' is certainly physical.

It would be a great mistake, and an insult, to regard archaeology as simply the study of broken objects and ruinous sites.
If people wish to denigrate the subject, they must not omit
consideration of its two most important manifestations, firstly
as work of art (already mentioned as the most deliberately
communicative kind of physical evidence) and secondly as the
study of human ecology. Because archaeology is concerned
with all kinds of physical evidence which are in any way connected with, or interpretable as, human history, it is also (or
should be) concerned with complete physical environments or
landscapes. It is essential for us to realize that the average
landscape does not simply carry or contain human artifacts:
it is *itself* an amalgam of man-made and natural phenomena,
because it is the scene of an ever-changing adjustment or contest
between man and nature. This is why the modern archaeologist sees his sites (whether buried or above-ground) as intimately related to the natural world of rocks, land-forms,
animal and plant life, climate and much else. Although the
archaeologist with his essentially human interests is mainly
concerned with the specifically man-made parts (what Carl
Sauer called the 'cultural landscape'), he is also concerned with
the natural background in so far as it helps to explain human
decisions and responses. In other words, archaeology in its
largest dimension is close to, and hardly distinguishable from,
historical geography, because they are both the study of place
– not for its own sake, but for the avowed purpose of throwing
light on human history. (See chapter 7).

Nobody would deny the importance of place in human life,
because man is not a disembodied spirit but an intelligent
animal who systematically exploits and moulds his physical
surroundings. Place is therefore much more than a list of man-
made and natural features: it is a unique blend of natural challenges and human responses. It is the way in which different

generations, using the technology available to them, have developed their settlements, food-economy, commerce, industries and communications on the basis of their predecessors' work and in response to the advantages which nature itself offers. In other words, these basically economic problems have stimulated an enormous amount of intellectual activity which is fossilized in the fabric of the landscape. The debate among psychologists and others on the precise role that the purely physical environment plays in the formation of human character will no doubt continue for a long time to come, but nobody doubts that it does make some difference whether one was brought up in a palace or slum, in town or country, in the mountains or plains, in space or confinement, in beauty or squalor. Nor, as the final and highest demonstration of the importance of place, should we forget how men of sensitivity have been inspired by the significance and qualities (not necessarily the beauty) of their surroundings to create great literature, painting and music. The interaction of place and mind is as subtle, varied and mysterious as the relationship between body and mind, and to write history without giving due attention to place, or rather man-in-his-place, is to present a sadly distorted view of the past.

It seems then that the basic difference between archaeology and history lies primarily in the subject-matter or raw material. Whereas the archaeologist is concerned with things, ranging from small objects to the total physical environment, the historian is concerned primarily with writings. However, this apparently easy distinction is a deceptive one. When one analyzes it further, and considers how history in the broad sense is constructed, the difference between the two kinds of evidence does not seem anything like so obvious and complete.

By definition, the historian is concerned with written documents. But what is a document? In its original form, it is a physical object (whether made of paper, parchment, vellum, stone, clay, etc.) and as such is part of the *archaeological* record. When historians examine documents as physical objects, and record their shape, size, condition, binding, seals and so on, they are, whether they admit it or not, behaving as archaeologists. The writing on a document, as a series of characters or signs, is also part of the archaeological record. For example, when a classical historian discusses the style of lettering on an inscription, or a medieval historian examines the ink used in a charter, he is clearly concerned, not with words as such, but with shapes and materials. The important science of diplomatic, developed by historians to test the authenticity of documents, has always placed considerable emphasis on physical characteristics (see p. 60).

If the document itself and the symbols on it are strictly archaeological, what is there left for the historian to call his own? There is of course the most important aspect of all, and potentially the most rewarding – the message or statements conveyed by the writing. It is the interpretation of these statements which is the true and distinctive role of the documentary historian. R. G. Collingwood summed this up by saying that the historian was concerned, not with documents, but with 'statements asserting or implying alleged facts.'[5] To interpret these statements and to assess the accuracy of the 'facts' the historian has developed special techniques, which will be discussed in Chapter 3.

A document, as already stated, can be made of several substances. The majority of manuscript and printed documents are of course on paper and parchment, but others, particularly in classical and pre-classical times, consist of more weighty materials like stone and clay. There is no essential difference between a paper document and an inscription on stone – both are archaeological artifacts which bear historical statements, and they therefore must be interpreted by the distinctive methods of both archaeology and history. While studying an inscription as a physical object, the archaeologist can derive information from the type of stone, the way it was worked, the kind of lettering, the find-spot, stratigraphical position and so on. The historian will study the inscribed message in exactly the same way as he studies a parchment or paper, to establish for example who wrote it, when, and for what purpose. It makes no difference that the pen has been replaced by a chisel or style, and the paper by stone or clay.

When an historian focusses attention on a statement, he is dealing with the recorded thought of a human being who lived in the past, that is to say, a thought which has been frozen or fossilized into writing. The statement may or may not be true, and the historian will try to assess its reliability as 'fact'. Even if it is untrue, it remains the personal expression of an historical person, and may still have significance as revealing, for example, a purpose, prejudice, or state of mind. It is worth remembering that the statement is the end-product of a whole train of thought and experience which will never be fully deduced. In other words, historical statements are the deliberate and conscious refinement of considerable anterior thought; they are designed to be heard or read, and there is always a motive behind them which the historian must try to recover.

When Collingwood described the historian's concern with statements, he pointed out that they need not always be written but can also be spoken. There is no essential difference between the two forms, because they are both verbal communications between human beings. There are, for example, people alive today (in the 1970s) who spent the first 20 years or so of their lives in the 19th century: therefore it is possible for historians to talk to people who actually remember the events of that period. Memory, clearly an important kind of historical evidence, is a mental store of thoughts and images which comes of direct personal experience, and involves no intermediary or external evidence between the person and the event concerned. Nevertheless, as we all know, the memory can play tricks, and the historian must therefore subject all reminiscences (other people's and his own) to critical analysis and comparison – like any other piece of historical evidence. Estyn Evans, for example, has warned from his experiences in rural Ireland that the inquirer must beware of the 'countryman's facility of speech, his poetic licence and his fatal desire to please'.[6] But he and others have shown that there are aspects of life in the recent past for which oral evidence and memory are specially suited, and for which written evidence is meagre or non-existent. Obvious examples are village customs and traditional crafts before the impact of war and industrialization.

Memory does not only relate to the recent past, and to the lifetime of living people: it is also an important ingredient of many written sources. For example, records like manor-court rolls were not actually written at the time of the meeting, and though they may be partly based on notes taken then, memory must also play a part in their compilation. Similarly, nearer our own time, many political biographies rely heavily on personal memory and reminiscence. Furthermore there is the phenomenon of a collective folk-memory, handed down orally from generation to generation. This was often recorded in writing at some later date, for example by medieval chroniclers, because it constituted evidence otherwise unobtainable.

Place-names are another good example of a blend between the written and the oral. They are basically spoken words, which have been used and handed down by successive generations. In course of time, the word has usually changed (perhaps to make pronunciation easier, perhaps as a result of changing language, dialect or race), and at intervals it may also have been frozen or fossilized into writing. The expert collects as many written versions of the name as he can find, the earlier the better. From these he can show how the word has evolved in every-day speech, and if possible its original meaning in the remote past.

With the exception therefore of the memories of living people, the historian is usually dealing with objects (documents), which fortunately for him have messages written on them. The archaeologist is surrounded by a much greater variety of objects, which carry no such messages. However, the hands and muscles which made artifacts and monuments, as well as those which wrote or inscribed documents, were guided by brain and intelligence. It follows therefore that the objects themselves are the expression of some kind of thought, and are to use Gordon Childe's phrase 'the concrete embodiment of thoughts'.[7]

Now if documents convey statements and thoughts, and if artifacts are the embodiments of thoughts, is there any real difference between them? There is indeed, and it lies in the character and range of the thoughts involved. The historical statement is the direct and accurate expression of a thought, in fact it *is* a thought in written form. It is also completely explicit. It says precisely what the writer intended to say, no more and no less (even if he said it badly or inaccurately). Perhaps most important of all, it can refer to literally any subject which exercises the human mind. It can be a simple, factual statement such as 'On May 20th 1620, the parish church was burnt down' or it can be a statement of a completely abstract and spiritual nature such as 'In the beginning was the Word, and the Word was with God, and the Word was God.'

By contrast the thought embodied in an artifact is only implicit or implied. It is not overtly expressed or articulated. In addition, it is severely circumscribed because it will only refer to the basic needs, motives and technical know-how which led to the production of the object. For example, the making of a simple tool like a flint scraper was probably controlled by thoughts about the animal to be skinned, the quality of the

hide to be scraped, the choice of a piece of flint, and the way
in which the maker had been taught by his elders to strike the
stone and then use it. The thoughts which an archaeologist
gropes for are therefore only approximate, and they are mainly
concerned with materialistic and technological considerations.
Written and spoken statements *can* express a range of intellectual and spiritual considerations, which material evidence,
even works of art, could never even approach. No object on
earth, not even the splendours of Sta Sophia or Chartres, could
ever express the philosophically-charged first words of St John's
Gospel. Nor, to take another example, can the crumbling urns
and bones which were in 1658 dug out of a wind-swept Norfolk
field come, as an expression of human thought and feeling,
anywhere near the beautiful book which they inspired – Sir
Thomas Browne's *Urne Buriall*. It has to be acknowledged that
words are potentially more efficient and versatile vehicles of
human thought than objects, but that nevertheless the latter
remain important historical evidence for those areas of human
life where verbal documentation is thin or non-existent.

By definition the archaeologist deals with physical objects.
Yet in practice, in order to extend his range of comparative
knowledge, he reads many secondary printed sources such as
excavation reports, museum catalogues and text books. As
Stuart Piggott has pointed out, the archaeologist 'has to spend
a surprisingly large part of his time reading the results of other
people's work; I reckon, as an archaeologist studying the
prehistory of Europe and the British Isles, that I have in the
course of a year to go through at least fifteen to twenty journals
dealing with our own islands, and sixty or seventy covering the
European continent. If you add marginal studies in history,
philology and Oriental archaeology, the total would naturally
be bigger, and, of course, does not include books and mono-
graphs'.[8] The archaeologist also gathers considerable knowledge by word of mouth. As publication normally lags years
behind work in the field, much new information is given orally
in conversation, lectures and conferences. In fact the end-
result of any archaeological research is not objects but words
– a written account of what was found and how this is interpreted in terms of human thoughts and history. So the archaeologist, whether he knows it or not, is trying to assess the reliability of the spoken and written word, and is therefore using
the raw materials and techniques of the documentary historian.

It may be objected that this analysis of the character of artifacts and documents is simply a play on words, and depends on the definitions one adopts. This is partly true, for one must accept the full implications of one's definitions, but the main purpose of the exercise has been to point out two vital facts. First, that there is indeed an essential difference between archaeology and documentary history: one deals with physical objects and the other with spoken and written statements. But secondly, that in spite of this basic distinction, archaeologists and historians have practical experience of each other's raw materials and methods. The historian, because life is not lived in a physical vacuum, inevitably comes into contact with material evidence, and frequently uses it for his own purposes. Similarly the archaeologist, in assessing the reliability and significance of written and spoken statements, practises history. This overlap of evidence and function emphasizes the essential unity of historical knowledge: there is really no justifiable way of making the worlds of the archaeologist and historian exclusive and self-contained.

2 The archaeologist at work – The interpretation of physical evidence

The purpose of this chapter is to consider further the character of physical evidence, and to see how it is actually interpreted and built up into an intelligible, historical account – how, in other words, history in the broad sense is extracted from the archaeological record. How can mute objects like potsherds, swords and post-holes be made to 'speak' of the way in which people lived in the past? How does the archaeologist reconstruct the actions and thoughts inherent in his material? Inevitably as with any discussion of the nature of archaeology, we shall be dealing largely with prehistory and quoting the work of prehistorians. This is certainly not to suggest that prehistory is synonymous with archaeology, but because it is in this sphere that one can best see archaeology at work on its own – in what Hawkes has called a 'text-free' situation.[1]

Let us briefly recapitulate the nature of the evidence. It consists of portable items (e.g. pottery, brooches and hand-tools) and immovable monuments (e.g. burial-mounds, field systems and houses). All these, large and small, are made by man from natural raw materials and are therefore by strict definition artifacts (i.e. the products of human craftsmanship). But we must also admit that archaeological evidence can embrace entirely natural objects which have had some connection with human life. These can be relatively small like animal bones, pollen grains, seeds, sea-shells and meteorites, or they can be large landscape features such as caves, primeval forests, gravel terraces and river valleys.

In normal excavation reports, one expects to find not only a record of the artifacts found, but also of their context, that is, the layers or stratification in which they were embedded. The principle of stratification will be discussed later, but it is worth commenting here that these layers can be either natural or artificial, or more often a mixture of the two. Natural strata consist of grains of weathered rock, laid down as a result of processes such as silting, wind erosion and the action of earth-worms; artificial strata are built up of the humus and debris of human occupation and economic activity. It should be remembered that purely natural layers can have great archae-ological significance, for example those which are sometimes interposed between occupation-layers in caves and rock shelters, and which represent periods of desertion. The undisturbed geological layer beneath a site, which archaeologists simply call 'natural', not only acts as a limit or frame to the stratification, but can be of direct help in deciding why the site was chosen in the first place. All strata in an excavation, whether natural, artificial or mixed, are a vital part of the archaeological evidence, because they add up to the total history of that site in terms of human use and abandonment.

Artifacts are, to use Childe's phrase again, 'the concrete embodiment of human thoughts'. Although these thoughts are implicit and have to be inferred by the archaeologist, they are none the less real and vital as historical evidence. It is because an artifact is the product of human thought or 'know-how' (as well as of manual dexterity) that it can be said to embody and represent thought – this is its only claim to have historical significance. In this connection the word 'thought' is of course used in a very broad sense, and covers needs, motives, technical knowledge, and the customs and behaviour which a society prescribes for individuals. It stands for any considerations which may have controlled or informed a person's mind while he was making an artifact.

THE PURPOSE AND MANUFACTURE OF ARTIFACTS

If an artifact was made for a purpose, that is, a particular use, then it embodies or enshrines that purpose or is its expression in physical form. In the words of L. Biek, an artifact is 'human purpose impressed on inanimate material'.[2] To pursue our earlier example further, the purpose in the mind of the maker of a stone axe was reasonably clear: 'I am shaping this imple-ment, so that it can be used to cut down trees efficiently.' Such a statement could be put in many different ways, using a great variety of words. This does not matter as long as the archaeo-logist by his own methods of empirical inquiry works to recover the essential intent or gist of the maker's thoughts. Later we must investigate these methods and the principles behind them, but at the moment we are still concerned with the nature of the evidence itself. Accepting the technological standards of the period and the normally accepted equipment of his society, the maker set out to produce an object which could perform a certain function. The maker may not of course have used the axe himself, and may have traded it to someone else, but the end-purpose remains the same. If the full historical significance of any object is to be realized, its purpose must be deduced. The vast majority of man-made things embody purposeful thoughts – design implies purpose, and purpose implies thought.

Usually we have no doubt when we are faced with a man-made, and therefore purposeful, object. There is, for example, no chance in the known experience of man for an arrowhead to be the result of natural processes, whereas there are plenty of analogies, both in contemporary and historically-recorded societies, to show that human beings are capable of making such a thing in order to provide an arrow with an effective tip. We judge that the object is too symmetrical, too fine and regular to be a product of nature. It should be remembered that decisions of this kind are not always made quickly, especially when man-made objects are crude, and when analogies are not easily found. Boucher de Perthes (1788-1868) provides a good example from the history of archaeology. Although he soon convinced himself that he was finding man-made axes in the gravels of the Somme valley, it took him a quarter of a century to begin to convert the world of scholarship. Nor should we forget that there was a time when purposeful objects like polished axes were explained as elfshot or thunderbolts.

However there are still objects which we are unable to accept as definitely man-made or definitely natural. The so-called 'eoliths', crude flaked stones found in Pleistocene and earlier deposits, are a case in point. In the earlier part of this century Reid Moir and others thought that eoliths were man-made, and they were supported by an International Commission, but now the general opinion is that these stones were naturally flaked. The fact remains that they are not distinctive or regular enough for accurate diagnosis. In a recent survey of the East Anglian examples, J. M. Coles has confessed that 'their verity as tools remains a considerable problem. . . We have very little information about the natural flaking processes available in East Anglia in early Pleistocene times ... no natural sources are known today which could do this under observation'.[3] In other words, there is insufficient analogous evidence. In general however such objects as eoliths are rare, and the experience and comparative knowledge of the archaeologist enables him with a high degree of probability to distinguish the man-made from the natural.

Much the same applies to field-monuments. The field-archaeologist soon trains himself to recognize man-made structures and earthworks, and to distinguish them from natural features. Man-made monuments have a form, pattern and regularity which nature in general lacks. But here too, the occasional confusion is possible. Take, for example, a line of stones on a hill-side; this could be the root of an early wall or a periglacial feature caused by the thawing out of a frozen subsoil. Archaeologists have acquired considerable expertise in these matters in the last 50 years or so, and although there do remain features which cannot be explained, they are far fewer than they used to be. About a century ago, for instance, it was possible for people to believe quite sincerely that Brimham Rocks in Nidderdale (Yorkshire) were a prehistoric open-air temple sculpted by man.[4] Nowadays archaeologists, geologists and others have no difficulty in agreeing that the rocks were shaped by natural erosion.

Once he has established that an object is man-made, the archaeologist must ask himself what purpose it served. There are some quite common objects in the archaeological record the purpose of which is not known. For example those attractive metal 'dodecahedrons', of which about 50 have been found in the northwest provinces of the Roman Empire, have never been satisfactorily explained, because there is no contemporary or historically-recorded analogy for them. They have been variously interpreted as candlesticks, sponge-holders, religious symbols, and surveying instruments![5] Neither has anyone yet discovered the purpose behind such monuments as the 'wall-passages' of the Pennines, which have the appearance of strongly-walled trenches with paved floor and originally a timber and turf roof.[6] Some of these problematical finds and sites are assumed to have had a 'ritual' (that is, religious or ceremonial) significance. In that event, they are charged with a symbolic purpose or meaning, virtually beyond recall – the thought involved was on too high an intellectual and spiritual plane,

and could only be expressed in speech or writing. We may
guess that they were connected with a belief in gods or spirits,
and that some sort of after-life was accepted, but apart from
this we know little or nothing.

Thoughts about the actual methods and techniques of manufacture are also enshrined in artifacts. In other words, behind
every man-made object lie certain principles that governed its
manufacture. In the case of a hand-axe, for example, there were
clearly thoughts and principles at work in the selection of a
suitable piece of flint, in the choice of a hammer-stone, in the
strength and direction of the blows delivered, and in the deliberate production of sharp and blunt surfaces. Before and
during manufacture, the maker had in his mind an idea not
only of what he was going to achieve, but of how he was going
to achieve it. Like a sculptor he saw an ideal shape locked up
inside his nodule of flint, and was working deliberately and
systematically to reveal it. Not only are thoughts about the
methods and principles of manufacture based on the talent and
experience of the individual, but the individual has been trained
in the industrial traditions of the society he lives in. Craftsmen have usually served a period of apprenticeship, when they
learn the character of the artifacts which society accepts as
normal, and the technical means of making them. A careful
study of artifacts should enable the archaeologist to deduce
the methods by which they were made – this is the very least
he should be able to do.

It is sometimes said that archaeological evidence does not
lie, but can be misinterpreted.[7] In an obvious sense this is true,
because such evidence is entirely mute and interpretative thoughts
are inferred by the student. But of course deliberate forgeries
do occur and have been recognized: witness as random examples
the Kensington Stone, the Ring of Nestor, the Glozel affair
and, as an anthropological example, the Piltdown skull.[8] The
forger begins with some knowledge of the period he is imitating,
and particularly its manufacturing methods; he is also aware
of the standards of the archaeological 'experts' he is trying to
fool, and the criteria which they use. He hopes to deceive
contemporaries (and with luck, posterity) into thinking that
the purpose of the object belongs to the past, whereas its real
purpose is obviously a modern one – namely to deceive or lie.
The task of the scholar, as always, is to ascertain the true purpose
and to interpret accordingly.

INTERPRETATION

The archaeologist unlocks the thoughts implicit in a physical object by question and answer: it is a logical device for concentrating the attention, and connecting thoughts in an orderly sequence. It is clearly important to ask the right questions: that is, questions which are relevant and which the evidence is capable of answering. For example, faced with any kind of uninscribed object, it is clearly foolish and illogical to ask the name of the maker, what language he spoke or to what race he belonged – only historical and anthropological evidence can provide those answers. An object like a work-a-day tool can only be used for simple inferences about its form, material, manufacture and function. One can ask, and have a reasonable chance of answering, such questions as: how was it made, what is it made of, what is its purpose, has it any parallels, and what is it associated with? What could we theoretically learn from the character of a single artifact, assuming that it was unstratified and had no associations? It was shaped, we have agreed, because the maker had certain needs and motives, and had inherited certain principles of manufacture, but if the purpose of, for example, a stone axe was completely unknown, how would the archaeologist attempt to discover it? He might proceed as follows. First he would ask himself how precisely the object was made. He would soon observe that it was heavy, carefully and symmetrically shaped out of a fine-grained rock, and provided with one sharp edge. If the edge was chipped and battered, he would probably conclude that it had been used for cutting some fairly dense material. Other questions and possibilities would follow. In view of the carefully worked shape and balance, is it not likely that the implement was originally mounted in a wooden haft? On closer inspection our archaeologist might notice a band of scratches and abrasions, which could have been caused by slight movement in a haft. If he subsequently made a copy of the axe and mounted it in a wooden haft, he would find that, provided he counteracted movement in the haft (by binding it with thongs for instance), it was effective in cutting timber. Concentrating again on the method of manufacture, he may find that the stone had been very delicately flaked, and then finished by grinding and polishing. So, by degrees, conclusions would be reached about the standard of workmanship, about the way in which the object may have been used, and about a suitable word to describe it.[9]

While studying an individual artifact, the archaeologist will inevitably ask himself whether there are other examples, and will systematically search for parallels in publications, museums, contemporary societies, and in the experience of his colleagues. Though there are unique objects in the archaeological record, in most cases parallels are found and comparative study is therefore possible. K. C. Chang has said that 'archaeology as a whole *is* analogy'.[10] Everywhere the archaeologist is certainly looking for just and trustworthy parallels, which can help him as circumstantial evidence in the interpretation of objects. Analogies range from natural principles and properties, such as the way in which flint fractures when struck, to observations of human behaviour in contemporary or historically-recorded societies. Sometimes analogies are studied by means of deliberate experiments: the use of a hafted axe on a measured area of woodland, for example, or the reconstruction of pottery kilns. Our archaeologist speculating about his axe would of course find that there are primitive societies, now and in the past, in which objects similar or identical to his were used as axes (though in other contexts, he will find them used as weapons and hoes). This will probably confirm him in the belief that the word 'axe' can be justifiably applied to this class of object.

As more parallels are found, more questions and possibilities will arise. The archaeologist may conclude that the cutting edge of his axe had been reworked, because its proportions and balance were different from the normal run. He may find that his example falls into a group of large, heavy, facetted axes, which are made of a distinctively fine-grained greenish rock. By examining a sample of the rock under a microscope, it may prove possible to classify axes more precisely according to the exact mineralogical structure of the stone. From this, our archaeologist may wonder whether it is possible to identify the source of the stone, and to track down the actual sites where such stone was quarried and axes roughed-out. Finally, knowing the origin of the stone and plotting the distribution of finds, he may be able to reconstruct the system of communications by which the roughed-out axes or finished products were traded across considerable distances.[11] And so by constantly speculating about his physical evidence, as individual specimens and as groups, the archaeologist is driven to ever more observation and comparison. It is important to note that the work at all stages is both descriptive *and* interpretative.

When the available material has been exhaustively 'questioned', the archaeologist will usually attempt to explain the patterns and connections he sees, and to weld the evidence into a general interpretation of life in the past. There are several terms which are being used to describe this kind of higher interpretation. It is fashionable now to talk of creating 'models', while American proponents of the 'new archaeology' describe the formulating and testing of 'propositions'. Whatever word is used, this process is the same: the postulation of a theory or scheme which appears to fit the known 'facts', and which, one hopes, will survive the finding of new evidence.

In order to marshal and classify his evidence, and to build up complicated interpretations, the archaeologist relies on two vital principles. The first of these is stratification, which was developed in the 19th century by geologists-such as William Smith (1769-1839), known as 'strata Smith', and later adapted to archaeology by such pioneers as Worsaae, Thomas Jefferson and Schliemann. It entails the careful observation of the relative positions and context of material objects; but more specifically because the principle is at its most telling in excavation, it involves the relative positions of the layers in which material objects lie. The second principle is typology, or the study of how the form of objects has evolved, which was developed by paleaeontologists in their classification of fossils. This provides a completely independent method of classification for objects which have no stratigraphical or other associations. Basically both methods are means of dating objects relative to one another.

It is important to note that both principles were borrowed at an early date from science. There is therefore nothing new about the connection between science and archaeology. In a sense it has always been inevitable because science is the systematic study of the physical world in general, and archaeology is a means of abstracting human significance from any relevant aspects of that world.

STRATIFICATION

In an excavation stratification exists if one layer vertically overlies another, or clearly cuts through it, when the overlying or cutting layer must be the later. Layers can be of almost any size or shape, and only rarely are they neatly horizontal. This is because life in most periods has involved the digging of negative features like ditches and pits, and the construction of positive features like buildings, banks and mounds. Such activities inevitably produce complicated and contorted layering. The depth below ground surface of layers or objects is no indication of relative age – a late pit, for instance, can cut through and beyond several earlier layers. On a site with complicated stratification, the archaeologist must observe soil changes accurately and record them meticulously, so that he digs only one layer at a time and notes all its contents. Correct excavation and observation should therefore enable the archaeologist to arrange in a relative time-scale all the layers of his site, and the majority (as we shall see) of their contents. Stratification is basically a means of dating, not absolutely in terms of years BC or AD, but relatively. While the word 'stratification' refers to the layers in the ground, the related word 'stratigraphy' describes the *record* of those layers.

The relationship between a series of artifacts and the layer containing them is an interesting one. On the whole one would seem justified in assuming that a group of artifacts genuinely within the same layer must be broadly contemporaneous, in the sense that they were deposited when the layer was forming. But of course, as every practical excavator knows, it is common for earlier things to turn up as well, and occasionally a layer, such as the fill of a ditch, may contain nothing but considerably earlier objects. This is because human debris is churned around in the soil, and can become incorporated as strays in any later human enterprise. For example it is quite common in Europe for prehistoric flints to turn up in Roman layers. In fact it is the least old object (or objects) which must be nearest to the date of the layer itself; it gives in other words a *terminus post quem*, which means that the date of the layer must be *after* the date of the objects' manufacture.

Where there are several artifacts in a layer, not only will the much earlier strays have to be discounted, but out of the broadly contemporaneous material, one will inevitably find that there are slight differences in date. Furthermore, some artifacts are much more precisely datable than others: for example the so-called Samian pottery of the Roman Empire can be more closely dated than various kinds of coarse pottery, and therefore it will usually be more useful for the dating of layers and structures.

To turn the last proposition inside out, it is theoretically impossible for an artifact to be later in date than the layer which contained it. This is because objects are incorporated *as* a layer is forming. In spite of this, however, it does sometimes happen that an object proves to be of more recent date than the layer in which it was found. This does not necessarily mean that the dating of the layer was wrong, for it is now widely acknowledged that objects (particularly small ones) can be introduced into a layer at a later date by various agencies such as the burrowing of small animals, the growth of tree-roots, and frost-cracking.

In theory it should be possible for an excavator to spot these intrusions, as there should be differences of soil-texture and colour, but in practice such small traces are easily overlooked, and no excavator can honestly say that he could spot them all. An interesting example of the dilemma caused by an apparent intrusion occurred in the 1950s at Wareham (Dorset).[12] The rampart around the town was sectioned, and appeared from the great mass of pottery within it to be pre-Norman in date. However, out of hundreds of sherds, ranging from Iron Age to post-Roman, there was one piece from within the bank which was probably Norman. The excavators had therefore to decide whether they should give the single late sherd its full value, or whether they should accept the overwhelming mass of evidence for an earlier date as outweighing a single 'anomaly'. After much controversy, which delayed the report for years, a pre-Norman date for the rampart was accepted and it was published as such.[13] This decision is surely understandable, and is justifiable as a statistical probability. Even though modern excavation techniques attain an increasingly high standard, they can never be completely foolproof and a later intrusion may not be identified. Cases of this kind underline how important it is to dig and record as meticulously as possible, and also to carry out excavations on a scale which is likely to give a reasonable sample of datable artifacts.

These anomalies are best understood when it is realized that a single object may have several different dates. It has a date of *origin*, when it was made. It also has a date-bracket which was its main period of *use*. Finally it has a date of *deposition* when it found its way into the ground, deliberately or accidentally. In most cases when they are talking about the date of objects, archaeologists mean the date of manufacture. Sometimes the three dates are so close that there is no historical point in isolating them, but at other times the dates can differ substantially. For example, coins can remain in circulation or be privately hoarded long after minting, so that the date of their final deposition in the ground may be decades or even centuries later than their date of manufacture. Also one should never forget that some objects, particularly those with aesthetic and financial value, are likely to be passed down from one generation to another as heirlooms before finding their way into some archaeological layer.

There is one kind of stratification which is especially useful to the archaeologist. This is when a group of different artifacts apparently represents a single deposit at a single date. Stratigraphically such a group of objects is within an obvious layer, usually a pit, and they are said to be 'associated' or 'in association'. A case in point is a human burial with its assorted grave-goods; these were almost certainly deposited in a grave-pit or tomb as part of a single ritual, and therefore one can assume that all the artifacts found were in contemporary use (though they need not of course be of the same date of manufacture). Hoards of metal-work, which may contain hundreds of objects representing scores of types, provide another obvious example of association. One assumes in general that the objects found in a hoard were in broadly contemporary use, but it is of course always possible for things of considerably earlier manufacture to be included. For example the average 'founder's' hoard, often contains broken and obsolete objects which were being scrapped as well as finished and near-finished objects which would have been for sale or barter.

In the building up of archaeological knowledge, stratification helps in three ways. First, it enables the archaeologist to date artifacts and structures relatively, according to the layers they were in. This is the way for instance, that the theoretical sequence of stone-bronze-iron, worked out by Christian Thomsen in the early 19th century, was actually substantiated. Secondly, stratification enables us to date layers and structures more or less absolutely, by means of datable artifacts found associated with them. (Ultimately of course the absolute dates are derived either from historical sources or from science.) If for example a coin of the late 2nd century AD is found embedded in the foundation trench of a building, then the building is late 2nd century or later. Thirdly, it is possible to date in absolute terms hitherto-undated or loosely-dated artifacts when they are found securely stratified with fairly precisely-dated ones. For example the dating of Romano-British coarse pottery gains precision when it is found associated with historically-datable things such as coins and inscriptions.

This threefold effect is important, because it means that an excavation is not only a means of working out the history of *that* site, but also perhaps a means of showing the date and cultural associations of undated objects, and making a contribution to general archaeological knowledge. All workers in archaeology are interdependent, and the highest standards are therefore of interest to more than the excavator and his site.

TYPOLOGY

The word simply means the study of types, and seems to have been first used by General Pitt-Rivers (1827-1900). In its purest form, typology involves the detailed study of artifacts (particularly their material, form and function), classifying them into recognizable types on the basis of their physical characteristics, and then arranging them in an evolutionary sequence. Human tools and weapons can be said to have 'evolved' as new materials have been discovered, as efficiency is improved, as they have become more complex, and as tastes and fashions change. Given a number of prehistoric axes or modern motor-cars, it should be possible to arrange them in a convincing sequence ranging from the technically primitive to the sophisticated, and therefore dated relative to one another.

Many artifacts show general resemblances, but also subtle differences; this is inevitable because individually-made things (as opposed to mass-produced things) are in the last resort unique. However, this last resort is not the prime concern of the archaeologist; he is interested in the rather more general features of his objects, which enable him to arrange them into classes or types with shared characteristics. At this level, it is assumed that similarities and dissimilarities reflect human cultures and industrial traditions. As the work progresses, the archaeologist may subdivide his main classes using subtler distinctions, but he will never subdivide to the absurd point where each object is in a class of its own. As Childe said, 'all types are abstractions obtained by ignoring the minor deviations of individual specimens'.[14]

Typology should be carefully distinguished from *taxonomy*, which is the related process of naming or labelling classes of physical objects and their characteristics. These names carry no cultural or chronological implications, but are convenient verbal 'handles'. Although the safest are basically descriptive (such as Corded Ware, microlith and causewayed-camp), a great number of these terms are much more interpretative of function, and run the risk therefore of being wrong (for example, pot-boiler, net-sinker, mortuary-enclosure and food vessel).

An object is of greatest significance to the archaeologist when it falls into a recognizable type. An entirely unique object, for which there are no parallels in form and ornamentation, is embarrassingly difficult to interpret. Can it be an example of a class which has otherwise disappeared from the record? Or is it the product of an individual craftsman who liked experimenting? In other words, is it an interesting historical accident, or a reflection of genuine cultural standards? Of course one should be able to comment on how such an object was made, but it will be much more difficult to explain its purpose because there are no analogies, and unless it was found in a stratified position it will be impossible to place chronologically and culturally. It sometimes happens that a unique object has considerable aesthetic merit. Although he is not trained in aesthetics the archaeologist will, one hopes, be impressed with artistic qualities, and will take them into account in his assessment of the way of life.

There are several dangers in the typological approach. In the first place, although one can often discern a sequence of types, one cannot always be sure of the direction of that sequence without an independent check. Devolution is possible as well as evolution; skills can be lost and diffused, as well as developed, especially where the march of ideas and fashion outstrips the spread of technical knowledge.[15] If therefore the direction of a typological sequence is to be properly established, it must be found independently by stratigraphy or some other means of scientific analysis.

When the typologist is studying a series of strictly functional artifacts, particularly those with cutting edges which are subject to improvement as new materials and methods are discovered, he is fairly safe in assuming a 'linear and uni-directional' progression. In other words, when someone works out a technical improvement, it is adopted generally – until in its turn it is superseded by a further advance. However, much typological research is not concerned with functional and technical improvements of this sort: for example in the study of pottery, the typologist is mainly concerned with differences of shape and decoration. Atkinson has warned that 'typology of this sort, if it reflects anything apart from the archaeologist's desire to bring order out of chaos must reflect mere changes in taste and fashion, which are notoriously fickle and unpredictable'.[16]

One of the greatest problems facing the archaeologist is that most artifacts surviving in museums were either found before modern techniques of excavation and recording were developed, or were found by accident. They therefore have few stratigraphic associations and if any historical significance is to be squeezed from them, intensive typological study (which includes statistical and scientific analysis) stands the best chance of succeeding.[17]

The differences between artifacts which the typologist finds may not always be a reflection of date (yet this is the main purpose of the exercise). They may be the result of individual brilliance or backwardness, or sheer accident. Other differences could be local and geographical rather than chronological. At its best therefore, typology can provide useful theoretical sequences, especially when dealing with strictly functional objects where the increase in efficiency is obvious. At its worst, it can degenerate into a sort of morphological madness, where distinctions and categories have no connection with the essential business of dating technical evolution or devolution.

Dating

Archaeology, like history, needs a secure framework of dates: if we are to have any chance of judging causes and effects, then we must have some way of arranging historical events in time. The two principles of stratification and typology do provide a system of relative dating, but that is as far as they can go. One may know that object A is earlier than object B, but one has no idea of when they were used in terms of solar years or absolute dates *Before Christ* or *Anno Domini* (to use the Christian calendar). Nor unfortunately do we know how long the objects remained in use. To answer the questions 'precisely when?' and 'for how long?', the archaeologist is therefore driven to seek non-archaeological means.

The traditional method is by cross-reference to sites and civilizations that are *historically* dated by documents. Written records have survived in Egypt from about 3000 BC, in Mesopotamia from about 2600 BC, in Asia Minor from about 1950 BC. Therefore it is possible to date objects by their association with documents which mention either the regnal years of known rulers, or actual dates by the calendar system then in use. These calendars and regnal years usually have some point of contact and overlap with the Christian method of dating, and can thus be converted satisfactorily though not always with utter precision into absolute dates BC and AD. When datable objects from a literate civilization are found in association with the artifacts of non-literate peoples (resulting from trade, looting, conquest, etc.) it becomes possible to give the latter absolute dates as well. Sometimes a long chain can be built up by the overlapping of cultures, and absolute dates can therefore be transferred hundreds and even thousands of miles away from the original literate civilization. This method of 'cross-dating', first developed by Oscar Montelius (1843-1921) when he extended Egyptian dates across Europe, clearly involves a blend of archaeological and historical evidence: the absolute date is obtained from a written source, and then transmitted geographically by the overlap and association of physical traits. Obviously the method is impossible for any period earlier than about 3000 BC.

Although this cross-dating sounds simple, it does not always work out so well in practice. It is not so easy to find genuine associations and overlaps, and each remove from the original dated object introduces further possibilities of error. For example, it may not always be possible to distinguish genuine 'imports' from types which simply resemble exotic objects. This then leaves the problem of explaining the resemblance. It is possible for a non-literate people to import a few exotic objects from their literate neighbours, and then start manufacturing copies and derivatives for themselves. As the copies may have a longer currency than the originals, it is clearly important to be able to distinguish one from the other. Again, objects belonging to a literate civilization may not themselves have a precise date, as their manufacture may cover centuries. Therefore the dates transmitted are in the form of a wide date-bracket. Nor should one forget the possibility that types can be independently invented in different areas. A one-way link, such as Mortimer Wheeler's finding of Roman pottery in a sequence of native Indian pottery, provides us with no more than a *terminus post quem*. The best examples of cross-dating, however, are those with links in both directions, such as the the undoubted Minoan-Egyptian two-way trade, because these prove contemporaneity.

In recent years various kinds of scientific analysis have provided new means of dating, both relatively and absolutely.[18] For the post-glacial period, we rely largely on palaeobotanists and the successive climatic and vegetational phases which they can work out from ancient deposits containing pollen and other plant remains. Crucial absolute dates are provided by such diverse methods as C14 analysis (measuring the dissipation of a radioactive isotope in organic materials containing carbon), dendrochronology (calculation of the age of timber by the counting and correlation of tree-rings), varve-counting (counting sediments which were deposited in an annual cycle) and thermo-luminescence (measuring the emission of light from heated particles in pottery). All these methods involve analysis by specialists of natural raw materials, which have either been used for making artifacts or are purely natural occurrences in archaeological contexts. The archaeological world is now engaged in the difficult task of adjusting to these new absolute dates: the older relative chronologies of artifacts and cultures are being pegged to the right tensions, and completely new and unsuspected relationships are being recognized. As McBurney has said, 'not only does this set the distribution maps into motion, affording a first indication of the place and time of origin, and direction of spread, but in the long run by bringing such processes gradually into sharper focus we may hope to discover something of the actual causative factors in the spread of ethnic groups and of culture complexes'.[19]

By way of illustration of the new methods, let us briefly trace the effect of C14 dating, the 'Libby revolution' as it has been called after its founder, on one period of British prehistory. As recently as 1954, it was widely accepted that the first agriculturists reached Britain about 2500 BC. In the late 1950s, however, C14 dates began to pile up, and made it seem that there were farming communities in existence by 3000 BC, some maybe as early as 3400 BC. Now tests with the long-lived Californian bristle-cone pines have called for a readjustment of the C14 dates, which have proved to be too low: some British sites may go back to *c.* 4000 BC.[20] This example serves to show how limited are the purely archaeological methods, when it comes to calculating the duration of cultures and periods.

It should be stressed that the new absolute dates are not precise to a year, but are time-brackets within which the true date is likely to lie. For example, when a C14 determination is expressed as 1610 ± 120 BC, it means that there is a two-to-one chance that the true date lies within the bracket of 1490 to 1730 BC. Because these dates do not give complete precision, some people prefer to describe them as 'chronometric' rather than 'absolute'. (See p.82)

HIGHER UNITS OF CLASSIFICATION

In an attempt to interpret their material evidence in terms of human actions and ways of life, archaeologists have, since the early 19th century, been much occupied in erecting schemes of classification and re-classification. The first unit invented was the *Age*. In 1816, when he took over the National Museum in Copenhagen, Christian Thomsen postulated the Three-Age system of stone, bronze and iron. The division was based on the different raw materials which Thomsen believed were used in *successive* periods for the manufacture of cutting tools and weapons. Excavation later proved his sequence to be correct. It certainly does not mean to imply that no flint was used in the Bronze Age, and no bronze in the Iron Age, but simply that for cutting edges the most advanced and effective material available was used in each period. Since Thomsen's day, others have added to and modified these large-scale units, so that the present terminology, to say the least, is not a masterpiece of logic.

Because stone implements seemed to fall into two groups, those that were finished by simple chipping and flaking, and those that were ground and polished, the Stone Age was in 1865 divided by John Lubbock into the Old Stone Age (or Palaeolithic) and the New Stone Age (or Neolithic). It was assumed, and later proved, that the ground and polished specimens were generally less old. Later still, it was found that these categories in their turn needed further subdivision. Among the unpolished stone implements, considerable development was apparent from very primitive types with early geological and stratigraphical associations to relatively sophisticated types.

Accordingly the Palaeolithic Age was subdivided into Lower (or early), Middle and Upper (or late). Because the major part of the immensely long Palaeolithic Age was appreciated as the human response to the geological Ice Age, and because there were clearly important changes of equipment in the post-glacial period (before polished implements were developed), a new era called the Middle Stone Age (or Mesolithic) was introduced by H. M. Westropp in 1866. To make things more complicated, the definition of the term Neolithic subsequently changed! Whereas it was originally used to denote the period when ground and polished implements were in use, it is now normally used to indicate a farming economy as opposed to the earlier food-gathering economy. Its first definition was therefore technological in character, and the second economic.

It will be noticed that when subdivisions occur they are frequently threefold – early, middle, and late. This is simply a logical device in order to distinguish the objects which never overlap from the objects which do. In other words, objects representing the early phase will occasionally turn up in association with those of the middle phase, and the middle with the late, but never the early with the late.

The 'Age' is still a valid technological concept, but it is crude and, as was realized before the end of the 19th century, has no chronological value because of the uneven spread in time and space of technical ideas. So there developed the idea of the 'culture', a smaller-scale unit which it was hoped would correspond more closely with actual human groups and societies in identifiable areas. The word has been variously defined. Childe called it 'a complex of regularly associated traits'.[21] The compilers of a recent Dictionary of Archaeology put it thus: 'if an assemblage recurs consistently over a restricted area and within a given period (i.e. has limited distributions in space and time) it is described as a culture, and taken to be characteristic of a particular human society.'[22] In other words if certain types of physical remains are found regularly associated and stratified together, then they are assumed to be the physical expression of a distinct society or way of life.

It is potentially possible to trace the geographical extent of each society by recording the distribution of distinctive artifacts and monuments. For many years now the distribution map has been part of the basic equipment of the archaeologist, and often it can be shown that a culture occupies a distinct geographical region. Of course the distribution of traits within the same culture should in general agree, and one needs a certain minimum number of finds before one can expect them to cluster in an intelligible and significant way. In this connection, it is perhaps worth mentioning that artifacts will sometimes stray beyond the strict limits of a culture as a result of, say, trade, whereas the monuments characteristic of a culture cannot stray. For example Roman pottery and other artifacts have been found in such places as India, Scandinavia and Ireland (all beyond the limits of the Roman Empire throughout its entire history) but Roman villas, roads and amphitheatres have never been found in such places.[23]

A culture should not of course be confused with a race. A race, because it is an anthropological concept, will only be recognized by distinct and recurrent traits in skeletal remains. Nor can we assume that a culture is the same thing as a tribe, a political state, a confederation, a legal system, or a linguistic area. It *may* coincide with any of these, but not necessarily so. The one certain thing about the identity of an archaeological culture is that it represents a common tradition in material equipment alone and even then only in that part of the material equipment which survives.

In practice there are often great difficulties in defining cultures, and a certain amount of guesswork and personal judgement is involved. Sometimes there are simply not enough recurrent traits for us to be certain that they represent a distinct way of life. What is more, the traits that do exist may only involve artifacts made out of a single raw material. Another serious drawback is that some recurrent traits may be found so widely that they have no diagnostic value. Take, for example, saddle-querns; these are found commonly among many prehistoric cultures, and historically and technologically they are of great significance showing that agriculture was probably practised, but as a means of defining any individual cultures they are useless. For this purpose, the best traits are not infrequently things which were expendable and even trivial. Pottery is a good example: it was made according to taste and fashion, and being breakable it is found in significant quantities.

Often it is extremely difficult to draw the line between differences that betray a change of culture, and those that represent change within the same culture which, if it lasts for more than a generation or two must slowly change and evolve.

In many instances it is very hard to decide where one ends and another begins.

Finally, cultures may overlap with one another not only chronologically but also geographically. The artifacts of a certain culture may turn up in other cultural areas. The archaeologist has to decide what social phenomenon or mechanism this could represent. If the number of such strays is not too large, then they could have resulted from trade or barter. If the objects are noticeably valuable, looting might be the cause of their removal. When large numbers of exotic objects are found, then there is the possibility of migration or conquest or federation. This kind of speculation is commonplace: it is frankly an intelligent guess based on existing evidence, and new finds may cause frequent re-assessment.[24]

The idea of cultures is obviously useful, even vital, to the organization of archaeological knowledge: the archaeologist must resort to some kind of grouping at this level, whatever term he uses, in order to arrange his material. At the same time it must be admitted that the culture is a crude device which gives only a rough approximation to the truth. As Stuart Piggott has said, 'to some extent the archaeologist has to decide as he goes along whether or not a recurrent assemblage of elements of material culture is large or significant enough to be dignified by the name of culture'.[25] Where he decides that he cannot use the term, there are alternatives – a bewilderingly large number in fact – such as sub-cultures, traditions, series, style-zones, groups and sub-groups. The word *industry* is commonly employed for assemblages made of the same raw material: in the Palaeolithic and Mesolithic where stone is practically the only material to survive and so much else has perished, it seems more reasonable to talk of industries and industrial traditions than of cultures.

So far we have been discussing the definition of cultures by the use of distinctive and recurrent traits (or type-fossils as some archaeologists have called them). There is, however, another method which has been used successfully, in particular by American archaeologists. This is based on the statistical frequency of various kinds of objects which are found in association. The frequency with which objects are found is surely as important as the fact that they occur at all. The great advantage of defining cultures statistically is that the archaeologist is not then entirely dependent on a few really distinctive traits:

he can study the assemblage as a whole, and objects which
occur widely in more than one culture may still have significance
in the frequency (or infrequency) of their occurrence. Because
it involves the inspection and counting of every scrap of evidence,
this method is naturally very laborious and time-consuming.

On the other hand, there are obvious weaknesses in the
statistical approach. In the first place the uneven and chancy
survival of archaeological evidence may well distort the frequencies and relative proportions of the various kinds of object.
On the whole the smaller, less valuable, and more breakable
an object is, the more chance there is of finding it in an archaeological context. In order to provide adequate statistical data,
far more types and examples of each type are necessary than
are usually found. In practice only stone artifacts, pottery and
animal bones are likely to occur in sufficient quantities for
meaningful analysis. Secondly, a great deal of care has to be
taken to allow for different frequencies on different kinds of
site. For instance the number of scrapers found in the excavation of a barrow will clearly differ from the number found in
a settlement of the same period. In any case, many more barrows
than settlements may have been excavated in a given area.
Furthermore the kind of excavation employed may also effect
statistical frequencies. Not only do excavations vary in extent
(some sites of limited size such as barrows are nowadays *totally*
excavated, but other large-scale sites such as settlements, caves
and hill-forts are in general only partially excavated) but there
are bound to be differences in the actual standards applied.
Recent work has suggested rather disturbingly that sifting can
make a difference of up to thirty per cent in the number of
artifacts recovered on Stone Age sites.[26]

THE SCOPE OF ARCHAEOLOGICAL EVIDENCE

Some archaeologists, like some historians, have seen the job
of historical reconstruction as falling into two distinct parts:
the collection of data, and its interpretation. In fact this dichotomy is totally unreal, as interpretative thought is involved at
every stage. In making inferences about the purpose of a hand-
axe, and the way in which it was made, we are interpreting;
similarly when we distinguish layers in an excavation, and
record the character and contents of each, we are mentally
processing observed data. The definition of a culture or the

sketching of the ecological history of an area is merely interpretation and generalization at a higher level.

How far, then, can the history of individual objects, whether
natural or man-made, help us to reconstruct the multi-facetted
history of human beings and societies? Some scholars insist
that physical evidence, though very useful for certain aspects
of human life, has distinct limitations beyond which it is impossible to go; while others, who see themselves as the apostles
of a 'new archaeology', believe that there are virtually no limits
to what we can reconstruct of the past. One American scholar
has recently said that by making and testing propositions 'it
should be possible to expand our knowledge of the past almost
indefinitely'.[27] Much of the argument turns on semantics.
When their utterances are analyzed, the conservatives do not
seem so conservative nor the revolutionaries so revolutionary.

The classic and orthodox statement of the limitations of
physical evidence was given in 1954 by C. F. C. Hawkes.[28]
He postulated that there were four main categories of information about human life, which get progressively harder to obtain
from physical evidence alone. First, inferences about techniques and technology are relatively easy. When an archaeologist
talks about the achievement of a community or culture as, for
example, craftsmen in stone or metal, or as house-builders, he
is making direct inferences from his evidence, and what he says
is in all probability historical truth. Secondly, it is fairly easy
for the archaeologist to move from technological to economic
considerations: how for instance a community subsisted on
food-gathering or mixed farming or on industrial specialization.
The third category of information is considerably harder to
obtain, and concerns social and political institutions. How
was the community governed? Was there a ruling élite, or a
single chieftain? Were there distinct social groups or classes?
What was the pattern of land-ownership? It is not that a physical
basis for such considerations does not exist, and that inferences
have not been drawn, but that the archaeologist's evidence at
this level is the indirect and inessential by-product of increasingly
abstract aspects of human life. Finally, inferences about spiritual life and religious institutions are the hardest of all. To this
one could perhaps add questions of individual personality and
intellectual achievement.

Those archaeologists who argue that there are no or few
limits to the human history which can be derived from archaeo-

logical evidence, usually work in fields where it is possible to find ethnological parallels – either in contemporarily-observed or historically-recorded communities which descend from those whose relics are being studied. They often overlook the fact that their interpretation relies heavily on verbal statements derived from ethnology, and not simply on inferences drawn from physical evidence alone.[29]

Clearly there are aspects of human life which archaeological evidence cannot reach. Even with a freak survival like the Tollund man, who was found preserved in a Danish bog, although we know what he looked like physically, that he met death by strangulation, and even what he ate for his last meal, we still know nothing about his personality, his intelligence, his social status, his religious beliefs, the events which led to his death, or the laws under which he was presumably condemned. Archaeology can tell us little about the higher intellectual achievements of man in the past, beyond sometimes outlining them in a general way. We know in some detail from documentary history how Newton discovered the law of gravitation and Einstein the law of relativity; what would we not give to know how and by whom fire was harnessed, the potter's craft initiated and metallurgy first practised! These, unlike other intellectual achievements, have left clear traces in the archaeological record but the personal history of the inventors and their work has vanished. By the use of new statistical and scientific techniques, and by the steady improvement of general standards, archaeology will undoubtedly penetrate deeper into human history, but the 'ladder of reliability' proposed by Hawkes remains a perfectly valid concept.

The kind of history which archaeology supplies is not unimportant, and is in fact very similar to that which interests the modern historian who tries to understand the economic and technological foundations of human society, on which the higher achievements (such as religion, literature, justice and philosophy) are based. As Sir John Clapham has written, 'of all varieties of history the economic is the most fundamental. Not the most important: foundations exist to carry better things.'[30] The modern archaeologist is primarily interested in the economic sphere of life – using this term in its widest sense. In fact it probably would be better to say that his approach is 'ecological'; he aims to study as completely as possible the relationship between human groups and their total environment

– geological, climatic, botanical, zoological and otherwise – because this is the highest kind of history which archaeological evidence is competent to reveal fairly *fully* and *on its own*.

THE SCIENTIFIC REVOLUTION IN ARCHAEOLOGY

In the last half-century or so, archaeologists have been making increasing use of a wide range of new scientific techniques. What is the effect of this 'scientific revolution'? Do the new techniques simply refine old methods and approaches, or do they actually replace them? More important still, have they in any sense revolutionized the basic aims and purposes of archaeology? Has science, in other words, widened the horizons of the archaeologist? These questions will no doubt continue to be debated for many years. Already many diverse opinions are being expressed, and as is usual in a period of rapid change some very extravagant statements are being made.

Among the scientific techniques that have added considerable refinement to typological studies we may mention the following. The microscopic examination by petrologists of the stone used in the manufacture of Neolithic axes has resulted in the much more detailed classification of these objects than was previously possible. Similarly the spectrographic analysis of bronze tools and weapons has revealed physical attributes unknown to the traditional typologist – for example the deliberate addition of lead, which now marks the transition between the Middle and Late Bronze Ages in Britain.

Other techniques like palaeomagnetic surveying and aerial photography are invaluable aids to field survey, and have led to the discovery of countless new sites and finds. The field archaeologist now has a much wider repertoire of methods to use, particularly for the discovery of buried sites which leave no surface traces.

It is in the field of dating that science has had its most revolutionary effect. With C14 analysis, dendrochronology and thermoluninescence, scientists have given the archaeologist something he could never provide for himself by traditional means – methods of obtaining absolute dates *directly from physical objects*. In a sense this vital information is latent within man-made and natural objects, and must be regarded as part of their potential archaeological character – but it can only be arrived at by highly specialized scientific techniques. We must see this potentiality as latent in all objects, although in most cases science has not yet provided techniques for its extraction.[31]

There are still other scientific techniques that are specifically concerned with natural phenomena found in archaeological contexts, and which therefore cast light on the natural environment surrounding human life in the past. This approach has been rapidly developed in recent years, and environmental appendices are now common in excavation reports. J. M. Coles has described the development thus: 'archaeology . . . has moved from a phase of pre-occupation with the material equipment of early man to an expanded study of man in his prehistoric setting – *the material equipment as it relates to the natural environment.* Environment, as used by archaeology, means a number of factors interrelated, a combination of climate, soil, fauna and flora, topography, and it is the study of these factors as determining or influencing the activities of prehistoric man that concerns us'.[32] (The italics are mine.) In practice this means that the total 'deposit' of an excavation (i.e. the soil itself and its constituent plant and animal remains such as seeds, pollen, bones, insect fragments, molluscs and human or animal faeces) is as valid as archaeological evidence as are cultural artifacts. The natural and man-made kinds of evidence are widely complementary: each is weakened without the context and stimulus of the other. There is no need to question the importance of the ecological approach, though its novelty tends to be exaggerated by some (for generations, archaeologists have commented to the best of their ability and knowledge on such things as climate, soils and topography).

A related aspect of the 'scientific revolution' is an increasing use of statistics. This means that numbers now bulk large in archaeological reports, and are frequently expressed in the form of tables, graphs, histograms and various other kinds of summary diagram. One recent report on the excavation of a Palaeolithic cave in Cyrenaica contains 250 graphs and statistical tables, as well as three very large, folding inventories.[33] Providing the results of such quantification are expressed in an intelligible way, greater precision of detail is surely a good thing. In 1968 David L. Clarke published the most powerful plea yet for archaeologists to make far greater use of modern systems of mathematical analysis.[34] The basic purpose is to identify regularities and groupings over the whole range of physical evidence, from the artifact type to the 'techno-complex'.

If the archaeologist did not in fact seize every analytical device that came his way, he would indeed be shirking his duty. However, when the regularities and groups have been isolated, there still remains the difficult but essential task of interpreting them as far as the facts allow in terms of human thoughts and actions – as history in fact, but what Clarke would call 'the integrating, synthesizing study generating models, hypotheses and theories'.

It is in connection with environmental archaeology that some of the more exaggerated statements are made. Some people see a polarization of opinion between those who cling to the traditional 'historical' and 'particularizing' methods and those who conceive archaeology as a branch of ecology. References are heard to the 'artifactual' school on the one hand, and the 'pollen and snail brigade' on the other. In less extreme but equally unwise terms, the editors of an important book on scientific archaeology have written that 'the knowledge of prehistoric peoples derived by scientific methods will before long overwhelm the information which has been gained from the study of artifacts in relative isolation'.[35] Whether the word 'overwhelm' was meant in a qualitative or quantitative sense, or both, it is surely unfair comment on the traditional structure of archaeology and the principles which have been laboriously established over many generations. Is one to assume for example that stratigraphical evidence is of declining importance? And are not many of the new scientific and statistical methods simply refinements of traditional typology and taxonomy? It would seem better to regard the 'new archaeology' as a natural development and evolution from the past. Because they study a segment of the physical world, archaeologists have always been bound to borrow and develop techniques and concepts from related disciplines. It is because of the greater pace of change that we are tempted to talk of a revolution; yet there is nothing to be gained by adopting an exaggerated posture of scientific modernism, and turning one's back on the achievements of former generations. Although it is not yet appreciated widely enough, the development of the 'history of archaeology' – associated above all with the name of Glyn Daniel – is a valuable corrective. It helps to emphasize that the present state of archaeology 'is clouded and conditioned by past archaeologies',[36] and that archaeologists, like historians, must try to understand how their predecessors worked *in order to understand themselves.*

In the attempt to justify archaeology as an independent and autonomous subject, and in their anxiety to become more scientific, many archaeologists have tended to deny that it has anything to do with history, or is in any sense historical. This rather pathological attitude is based on a profound ignorance of what history is. It should be obvious enough that all the ostensible objectives of archaeology fall within the sphere of history (in the broad sense) and are of professional interest to many documentary historians: first, the reconstruction of cultural history; secondly, the description of how people actually lived in the past; thirdly, the delineation of cultural processes or regularities in socio-cultural life; fourthly, human life in its fullest ecological setting. All these overlapping aspects of life, ranging from the simple event such as the manufacture of an artifact to the complicated interpretation of cultural changes, are subsumed within history – as the record of human life in the past. The crude and blinkered view of some archaeologists, that the generalizing and processual character of archaeology can be clearly differentiated from the descriptive and particularizing work of documentary history has been brilliantly exposed by B. G. Trigger.[37] Documentary history (i.e. history in the narrow sense) involves interpretation at all levels, and like archaeology is both particularizing and generalizing. If archaeologists are so desperate to demonstrate their independence of documentary history, then they must go back to first principles, and found a convincing philosophy on the crucial difference between things and words.

Extreme statements are only a rationalization of personal preferences and prejudices, and the best that can be said of them when applied to archaeology is that they may cause us all to think more about the nature of the discipline and the effect that science is having on it. It is highly dangerous to suggest that archaeology is either exclusively historical or exclusively scientific, because it is of course both. Simply because the techniques applied to it are becoming ever more scientific, and because concepts and interpretations are being borrowed from both the natural and social sciences, it does not mean that the basic objectives of archaeology are any less historical, or that archaeologists will cease to talk of artifacts, monuments and cultures. It is vitally important that the increasing use of science in archaeology should not blind us to the historical objectives of interpreting and explaining human experience. If archaeology does not remain both scientific *and* historical, it will become sterile; with no historical objectives, it will become, in Jacquetta Hawkes' words, 'a vast accumulation of insignificant, disparate facts, like a terrible tide of mud, quite beyond the capacity of any man to contain and mould into historical form'.[38] On the other hand, without scientific methods and concepts, it will become vaguely and weakly humanistic; it will not have made use of the full potential of the available evidence. Perhaps R. J. C. Atkinson has summed up the debate best by saying that 'our aim should be no less than to permit archaeology to train upon the problems of man's history the full armament of his science'.[39]

3 The historian at work – The interpretation of verbal evidence

In conversation nowadays the historian's work is usually defined as the study of the human past from documentary sources alone. We have tried to show in the first chapter, however, that his basic conern is more specifically with statements or messages. In other words, his raw materials are the thoughts written and spoken by human beings in the past. Another point to emerge was that to understand the message fully, the historian must also consider the document as a physical object. It is the purpose of this chapter to consider in detail how the historian operates – how he, in his turn, wrings history in the broad sense from his documents, as both messages and objects.

It must be conceded that when one compares a theoretical definition of the historian's work with the way it is often practised, a great anomaly soon becomes evident. As history is commonly taught at various levels (in schools, colleges and universities), it appears to be based, not on original documents at all, but on such things as text-books and articles – that is, on the work and opinions of historians. Indeed one suspects that there may be a few academic historians who have never used an original document in their lives. Admittedly anyone interested in history must start by reading and absorbing the work of a great number of historians, past and contemporary, before he can hope to make his own necessarily small contribution to knowledge. What it is so easy to forget is that all 'facts' and opinions are *ultimately* based on the original writings and sayings of people in the past.

In no other academic subject is the foundation of knowledge so commonly overlooked, or the foundation and superstructure so frequently confused. So much emphasis is put on periods and problems, and on the conflicting opinions of historians, that the actual means of gathering evidence and creating new knowledge are often forgotten. There is certainly no other academic discipline where the average student is so divorced from practical research techniques. Can one imagine a student of chemistry graduating without a considerable amount of time experimenting in the laboratory? Is it possible to qualify as a geographer without some experience of field-work and surveying? Can a student of archaeology hope to master his subject without visiting museums, handling material, and working on excavations? True, the average student of history is instructed in the use of a limited number of secondary printed sources, usually as part of one year's special subject, but he is still given little or no opportunity to see, and work on, original documents, or of learning ancillary skills such as palaeography and diplomatic. One consequence of this is that when a post-graduate is faced with the task of doing original research, he finds himself unprepared and untrained both intellectually and technically.

In dealing with a certain historical subject, a teacher will mention many 'facts' and opinions, but he cannot be expected to give references to original sources for all of them, or to go through a critical discussion of each source. In practice he makes reference to certain scholars and their printed works, often stressing differences of interpretation. To this extent the student is obviously dependent on processed and second-hand information. But there is no reason why the student, in G. R. Elton's words 'must *essentially* take *all* his information at second hand' (my italics). There is no basic difficulty in teaching at least some history from original sources. In fact some exposure to documents is vital, for it makes both teachers and students much more conscious of the craft of history – that is, the pursuit of truth in human affairs by a patient analysis of verbal evidence. History without reference to sources is either a boring recital of so-called 'facts', or a generalized account of debates among historians. By contrast, one un-doubted reason for the popularity of archaeology in the last 25 years has been the direct contact it gives with the raw material and methods of the subject.

In the light of modern developments, there is no reason for perpetuating this complete reliance on the second-hand. The rise of the archival professional, the creation of new record offices, the depositing of vast collections formerly in private hands, the calendaring and cataloguing of many documents, technological inventions like photocopying and microfilm, these and other factors provide the student with a greater opportunity than ever before to see and use a certain amount of original material.

In rather the same way as the methods of archaeology are represented in their purest form in prehistory, so it will be noted that the methods of history are most easily and clearly demonstrated in the study of the Middle Ages – indeed they were to a large extent originally developed for it. This is one excellent reason why medieval studies must never be dropped from historical syllabuses, and why every student should have some contact with the period.

TABLE SHOWING STAGES IN DOCUMENTARY RESEARCH

1 *Definition* of subject – possibility of later re-definition as work proceeds.

2 *Discovery of sources* – manuscript, printed, inscribed, oral or from direct memory – records and chronicles.

3 *Palaeography* and transcription.

4 *Translation* of language.

5 *Diplomatic*, assessing the genuineness of documents – also the restoration of copied texts.

6 *Analysis* and interpretation of individual statements within documents.

7 *Synthesis* – grouping of facts – working out of new facts – the final shaping of the overall interpretation and its writing.

There are many books available which deal with historical method, but curiously very few seem to break the work down into its very simplest elements.[1] These may seem abundantly obvious, and in practice the process is often done automatically, but in any practical analysis its stages should surely be mentioned. There seem to be at least seven basic steps which the historian must take in the gathering and treatment of his evidence. First he must define his subject as closely as possible, and then remain prepared to re-define it if necessary, while his work is in progress. Secondly, he must continually search out the documents relevant to his chosen field of study, a process which has been described as Heuristic (from the Greek, meaning 'discovery'); thirdly, he must read the characters or alphabet; fourth, he must translate the language; fifth, he must establish whether or not the document is genuine; sixth, he has to analyze and interpret the individual statements of his sources and 'squeeze' them of their historical significance. Lastly, all the processed 'facts' are synthesized into an overall argument or interpretation. This is a logical progression, which involves carrying out these tasks in a set and irreversible order. Of course, some of these tasks often cost the historian little or no effort – he may for example be reading documents in his own familiar alphabet and language – but each document must theoretically be subjected to this kind of analysis, and usually there is something to be done at each stage. (See table opposite).

FINDING THE EVIDENCE

Before an historian begins to work at all, he must select a field of study. This is partly a question of personal inclination, partly a question of training, competence and experience. By reading the published work of former historians relevant to a certain area of history, he will become familiar with the existing state of knowledge, soaking up all the information he can find, and paying considerable attention to references and sources. In the course of this reading, it may become apparent that there are important gaps, ambiguities, or even outright contradictions, which suggest that the subject as a whole (or part of it) needs re-examination, particularly if, as is often the case, new evidence is known to be available. Right from the start, therefore, the historian is thinking interpretatively, not of course with preconceived ideas of what he is going to find, but always probing into the logic and significance of what others have written.

Within his chosen terms of reference, the historian will look for original sources in all the obvious places, and then in the less obvious, in an attempt to find anything which is relevant. Those used by other historians will be checked and studied afresh, and new ones sought out. Every effort will be made to see that nothing pertinent is overlooked, because the accidents of time have already pruned the evidence, and the historian must not further alter the balance by arbitrary personal selection. If he finds more documentation than he bargained for, then he might well have to cut down the field of study, or rely

on statistically sound sampling; conversely a paucity of evidence
may lead him to expand his terms of reference.

But where does the historian actually find his documents?
The short answer is, anywhere. They may turn up in out-houses,
damp cellars, dusty attics, or in jars hidden in caves. In practice
though, there are some places which are more obvious than
others. There are the national repositories such as, in Britain,
the Public Record Office and the British Museum. On a more
local level are county record offices, and libraries run by local
authorities, universities and learned societies. Manuscripts
can also turn up in private hands, government departments,
legal offices and commercial firms. Success in the search for
relevant material largely depends on the work done by archivists, bibliographers and other scholars in preparing indices,
catalogues, lists and calendars (summaries). Without such help
the historian's work would be immense, sorting through masses
of disparate material in the vague hope of finding something
useful. The average historian is unfortunately not in the happy
position of H. H. Bancroft (1832-1918) the historian of the
Pacific States of America, who simply bought up vast quantities
of documents and then hired an army of transcribers to work
on them!

It should never be forgotten that historical evidence now
includes completely new materials such as photographs, film,
tapes and gramophone records. These are mechanical means
of 'capturing' the sights and sounds of historical events as
they actually happened, and they enable us therefore to reconstruct the past with greater realism and immediacy than is
normally possible. Witness for example the power and horror
of the film which recorded in its wild flickering way the as-
sassination of President Kennedy. Whether the event is
unexpected or planned, the camera or microphone is not simply
an automatic and precise witness, but is always to be seen as
under the control of an operator who has techniques, interests
and motives.

What many people think of loosely as original documents are
in fact secondary. For generations, printed and edited versions
of documents have been used by students and researchers,
and they are an inestimable boon. In some cases documents
have been transcribed, in others both transcribed and translated.
In the study of national history they are particularly valuable,
as they make key documents readily available in printed form.

One thinks for instance of the work in England of the Record Commissioners, founded in 1800: they published the texts of Domesday Book, the Hundred Rolls, Inquisition of the Ninth, Valor Ecclesiasticus and many other basic sources. There is also the valuable work of national societies, many of which were founded before 1900. Some such as the Camden Society have wide-ranging interests; others such as the Selden Society (legal history) and the Hakluyt Society (travel and discovery) cover more carefully defined fields. In addition there are record societies for limited geographical areas, such as the Chetham Society (publishing from 1844 for Lancashire and Cheshire) and the Staffordshire Record Society (publishing from 1880).[2] Again, certain scholars have printed personal collections – Bishop Stubbs' famous *Select Charters* and more recently the volumes of *English Historical Documents*, come to mind. In the last few years there has been a sharp increase in the number of publications, which either consist entirely of printed documents or include them as appendices.

All these publications are invaluable aids to historical teaching and research, but the one thing about them which should never be overlooked is that they have been processed by a third party, who has selected, transcribed, translated and edited the material. So often have we all used such publications that we can easily forget that they are *not* the real thing. Even with a scrupulously accurate editor, there are features of the original which are not reproduceable: most obviously we lose the document as an archaeological artifact, and have to rely on the editor for his observations on such features as handwriting, condition, pagination and binding. More important still is the fact that the editor may not have done his job properly, and the actual message is therefore to some extent corrupt. Editors have been known to make alterations in the order of words, to omit sections, to restore illegible words, to translate very freely, and so on – all without explanation and warning. Nowadays, mercifully, the rules of editing are tighter and more widely accepted, but mistakes still occur. Even with a well-edited text, there remains the vital fact that an editor is interposed between us and the historical mind we are studying.

One other kind of secondary source worth mentioning here is the calendar. This is a summary or abstract of original documents. Here of course one is even further from the original, because considerable personal choice is involved. A calendar should be regarded, not as a substitute for original documents, but as a useful guide to their contents and whereabouts. Needless to say, a good index to subjects, persons and places is an important ingredient. The value and limitations of this kind of source are well demonstrated by the famous *Calendar of Letters and Papers of the Reign of Henry VIII*, originally catalogued in Victorian times by James Gairdner and J. S. Brewer, and revised in the 1920s by R. H. Brodie. This large collection consists of 21 volumes and summarizes more than 7,000 documents. It refers chronologically to most of the documents that were known at the time, and is widely used by students of 16th-century English history. Professor Elton has pointed out that although the transcriptions are done competently there are two serious disadvantages.[3] First, the calendar gives a 'quite misleading impression of completeness'; for in fact the originals are selections from many different sources and collections. Secondly, the editors arranged the material chronogically, and destroyed the original arrangement. As Elton laments, 'the provenance of documents – the way in which they came to be produced and deposited – is one of their most telling aspects, and this is something that, disastrously, cannot be established from that calendar.' In other words, an important aspect of the physical evidence has been lost. Unfortunately the originals at the Public Record Office were subsequently rearranged and re-bound, following the arrangement of the calendar!

Although the historian uses a considerable amount of evidence at second hand in the form of transcripts, translations and abstracts, the bulk of his secondary evidence is different again: it is existing historical knowledge and opinion – all the work done in his field by other historians, in the form of books, articles, lecture notes, or whatever. This is usually the starting point of research, and one returns to it repeatedly. Creative analysis of original sources is the essence of history, but this has to be constantly measured against, and related to, the work of other historians, both past and present. New research is, in other words, suggested and conditioned by earlier historical writing. In some cases the new is an amplification of the old, or simply a more detailed exemplification of general principles established by earlier writers, but often there is an important shift of interpretation, which involves the abandonment or serious modification of earlier opinions. It would be a rash historian who did not check the facts and interpretations of his predecessors by looking up at least some of the sources quoted, though there is of course always a certain amount of peripheral information which is accepted on trust. Every fact cannot be verified, but at least the general trustworthiness of other writers can be sampled. Finally, because so much depends on the work of one's predecessors, it is as important to give clear references to secondary sources as it is to primary – a rule not always observed.

While his work is in progress, the historian will naturally keep in touch with other people working in the same or related fields. Sources of information, which can turn up in the most unlikely places, can be exchanged, and different interpretations discussed. As in any subject, it can be very helpful to test one's ideas on someone else whose opinion one respects. It is also a very selfish and misguided historian who never notes down information and references which may be of use to other people. After all, a lot of information is simply 'stumbled across' rather than systematically found. Personal contacts are all the more important when information is exchanged in advance of publication.

TRANSCRIPTION AND TRANSLATION

The second stage in the historian's work is one that always has to be carried out, whether consciously or unconsciously. He must teach himself to read the words on his document as a system of letters or symbols. In other words, he must learn the alphabet and the script. In most cases the alphabet is a familiar one, but occasionally the historian is faced with an unknown script which has to be laboriously interpreted as ideas, sounds, syllables and words. The key to unknown scripts has usually proved to be inscriptions where the same message is repeated in two or three different forms, of which one is already known: for example the famous Rosetta stone, found at Rashid (Egypt) in 1799, has the same message, a decree passed by an assembly of priests in 196 BC, in two languages and three scripts. The first two versions are in Egyptian, using hieroglyphic (picture-writing) and demotic (a cursive script); the third version is Greek in the form of ordinary uncials, and this was the key by which the other two scripts were eventually transcribed through the joint efforts of Thomas Young,

François Champollion and Heinrich Brugsch.[4] Perhaps the most brilliant decipherment of all time was Michael Ventris' work on the Linear B alphabet and script – without, it may be noted, the benefit of a bilingual inscription.[5] The documents in question were inscriptions on clay tablets, found on Mycenaean sites in Greece and Crete. By studying closely the way in which the symbols were grouped, and making some brilliant intuitive guesses, he was led to the conclusion that the symbols stood for the syllables of a primitive form of Greek. Of course to do work of this sort, people like Ventris have to be logicians and linguists of a very high order, but essentially the clay tablets remain historical documents and their decipherment is an extreme kind of palaeography.

In many cases, the problem is not the decipherment of a strange alphabet, but simply reading an unfamiliar script in a known language and alphabet. A document more than, say, two or three hundred years old is likely to contain significant differences in handwriting, which have to be understood before the message can be gleaned. An obvious example is the long 's' which survived well into the 19th century. In any non-contemporary script, the student runs the risk of confusing certain letters which are closely similar. For instance, in reading the Secretary Hand of the 16th and 17th centuries, beginners are likely to mistake 'e' for 'o', 'c' for 'r', and several others in small and capital forms. Before that date the difficulties are much greater, even if we disregard the use of medieval Latin; the scripts used are further removed from the modern style, and there are numerous abbreviations, contraction signs and other symbols. Fortunately to help the student, there is an ever-increasing number of publications which explain the various characters, abbreviations and 'confusibilia'.[6]

There is a further aspect of palaeography which is important. At all periods there have been people who have written indistinctly or in a highly personal manner. This is one reason why palaeography cannot be regarded as an exact science: although there are conventions which are common and widely practised, one is always encountering personal idiosyncracies. At no period has handwriting been absolutely standardized. In some cases it may take the historian a long time to work out the characteristics of an individual's style, particularly in personal documents like letters or rough notes. Sometimes, as in the case of Samuel Pepys, writers used a personal kind of

shorthand which makes transcription even harder.[7] When
one is 'stuck' over a word, it often seems best to leave it for a
time: it may reappear in more legible form a second or third
time in the same document; again, by simply moving on and
returning later with a fresh eye, one sometimes understands
what was at first a meaningless squiggle. However, even the
most experienced historian and palaeographer is sometimes
beaten, and has to admit in a transcript that a word is (to him)
illegible or uncertain. It is better to confess failure than to
mislead others with a surreptitious guess which could be quite
incorrect.

The third stage in the historian's work is the translation of
language. In most cases this presents no great problem, as
the historian is studying documents in his own language, or
in a foreign language which he has learnt. It should be remembered, however, that one is in fact concerned with the language,
not of the present, but of some period of the past: even one's
own language a century or so ago had subtle differences of
meaning and style which have to be appreciated by the dis-
cerning historian. Furthermore, one may encounter other
subtleties which have a regional basis (that is, dialect), or even
a purely personal basis (where individuals have used language
in an idiosyncratic way). In practice of course one often trans-
lates while reading the script – in other words transcription
and translation are done at the same time. Nevertheless it
is right to consider the linguistic problem separately, because
it is essentially different from palaeography. This is well
illustrated in the case of medieval court rolls: each word has
to be appreciated as a collection of symbols, before we can
be confident of its meaning and place in the message. Furthermore, even though we may have read a word, we are often
obliged to hunt for its meaning in a medieval Latin word-list.
In the first stage one is concerned with individual letters and
signs, and in the second with vocabulary and meaning. The
point is even better made in the case of Etruscan inscriptions.
As symbols these are easily transcribable, but as language they
are virtually untranslatable.[8]

DIPLOMATIC
Up to now, we have been purely concerned with the problems
of finding and reading documents. The fourth stage is con-

cerned with establishing their genuineness or otherwise, and to do this historians have been developing for several centuries a special body of knowledge and techniques called diplomatic. As the name implies, this science was originally concerned with the critical assessment of official documents, particularly charters (or diplomas) which gave title to various possessions and privileges. But it can be, and is being, applied on a wider scale to many other classes of records, because basically it is no more than a logical enquiry into their internal and external consistency. Some of the crucial points are historical because they deal with the message, but others being concerned with various physical characteristics are archaeological in character.[9]

Taking the whole span of recorded history, documentary forgeries are comparatively rare. The majority of known examples were done in the Middle Ages, not usually as deliberate pieces of dishonesty, but to supply evidence for possessions, rights and claims which were otherwise regarded as well-founded. In other words, documents could be fabricated to support truths as well as untruths. It almost goes without saying that a forgery is still a significant piece of historical evidence and one wants to know who wrote it, when, and for what purpose. Diplomatic is not therefore a means of weeding out and rejecting worthless documents: it is a means of assessing whether a document is what it pretends to be. If it is not what it pretends to be, then it can be used and interpreted only in the light of its true nature, in arriving at which we must delve into the personality and interests of its true creator.

There are two main ways in which a document can be assessed. First, it should be consistent within itself. It should not, on any crucial historical point, contradict itself. (This is not to say, of course, that if the same word is spelt in several different ways, the document is bogus. Consistency of spelling has only been a *desideratum* in the last hundred years or so.) Secondly a document should be consistent with available external evidence. If in certain statements it flies in the face of all other evidence, which in character and volume seems acceptable, then one would begin to have serious doubts about its authenticity. For example, if it could be shown that at the date mentioned, one of the people who allegedly signed a charter had not yet been born, then forgery is more than likely. In this case, the comparative information about the witness and his life-span would come of course from other documents;

if several such records agreed about the witness' dates, this would tend to make the forgery more obvious. To a certain extent therefore, the quantity of genuine, independent evidence for a point is important, as well as its quality.

On the archaeological side, there are many features which could lead to the detection of forgery. It may be that the document itself, as an object, is anomalous in some way – in material, size, shape or condition. For example a paper document in England purporting to be 12th-century would be immediately suspect, because in general paper did not become available until the 14th century. Occasionally an erasure can be seen on a genuine document: thus, in 1368 a genuine charter of Richard I, giving the privilege of maintaining a gallows at Fyfield to the Abbot of Bruern, was fraudulently altered: the word 'Fiffehida' was erased, and 'Estlech' inserted.[10] This kind of physical detection may well be facilitated by various scientific aids and techniques, among them ultra-violet light, microscopes and the chemical analysis of inks.

An important aspect of the physical evidence is the actual nature of the handwriting, particularly the way in which individual letters are formed. The style changes according to periods, individuals, government departments and courts of law, and this simple fact forgers often forgot. For example Henry Coppedale of Beverley in 1376 arranged the fabrication of a deed which purported to be of 1293, but, unfortunately for him, it was done in a clearly late-14th-century hand.[11] This is a field where palaeography melts into diplomatic – where differences in handwriting are used for critical and dating purposes.

Under the general heading of diplomatic could be mentioned the restoration of ancient texts which only exist in the form of later copies.[12] There are many historical and literary works which come into this category, mainly from Classical and Medieval times. For a whole variety of reasons, copyists did not necessarily transmit the exact form of the original: some were simply careless and made little effort to understand what they were copying (there was always for example the possibility of the scribe mis-hearing, if he were being dictated to); some scribes deliberately added words or punctuation which they thought improved the text; others left out sections which they thought unimportant. If therefore these texts are to be used for a serious historical purpose, they have to be carefully studied, criticized and restored – 'a kind of cleaning and mending' as Langlois and Seignobos called it. The textual critic will see how copies have often derived from one another, and may be able to postulate a 'stemma' or family-tree. It will not necessarily be the earliest copy which is nearest the original, nor does a great number of versions for a particular reading mean that it is the correct one, but by a patient study of all the independent versions, and by subjecting them to criticism on all relevant grounds (language, handwriting, consistency of thought and style, knowledge of the period, possible confusions, dating, etc.), a purified text is slowly restored, word by word, sentence by sentence. (See pp. 110-12)

THE INTERPRETATION OF STATEMENTS

Diplomatic criticism is clearly interpretative and can involve highly sophisticated reasoning but, important though it is, it represents only the beginning of full historical criticism. We certainly need to know whether a document is genuine or forged, or whether a copied text contains later corruptions and interpolations, but now this critical approach must be developed further and used to assess the truthfulness and accuracy of the document, both as a whole and in its individual statements. Perhaps one of the best ways of doing this is to think in terms of the writer's involvement with the subject described. In other words, the historian must inform himself as fully as possible about the origin of the document itself, because on this depends the quality and significance of each individual statement contained in it. He starts by considering quite basic questions which may well have been asked already in the 'diplomatic' stage. First of all, *who* wrote the document? This does not mean just finding out a name – very often one cannot name the writer – but the kind of person involved, and particularly his or her position relative to the events described. In other words, the simple question of who? develops naturally into a consideration of why the document was written, and how the writer acquired his information. Secondly, *when* was the document written? The answer to this is usually the easier of the two, because documents quite often have dates written on them, and providing there is no reason to suspect error or forgery, one generally accepts what is offered. Where a document does not bear a written date, the historian may be able to judge it, if only approximately, by reference to certain key statements in the text. For example there may be some mention of events which are independently dated. Or there may be a chronologically-significant formula such as *exceptis viris religiosis et Judeis*: this would date an English deed to the period 1279-90 because the exclusion of 'religious men' is the result of the Statute of Mortmain in 1279, while the expulsion of the Jews by Edward I in 1290 gives a *terminus ante quem*.[13] On the other hand, there may be 'archaeological' means of suggesting a date, such as the style of handwriting or association with other dated documents. The main purpose of establishing the date of a document is to measure its temporal relationship with the events described. The general assumption is that the nearer the document is to the events, the more likely it is to contain *some* reliable, first-hand information.

Dating is not always as easy as simply reading 'May 16th, 1788'. One has to familiarize oneself with the regnal years of kings, queens, bishops, abbots and so on, with saints' days, and the difference between the Julian and Gregorian calendars. One has to know, for example, that January 1st was not accepted as the beginning of the year throughout most of medieval Europe until the 16th century, and in England not until 1752. However it is far easier to master these intricacies – especially with the help of various manuals[14] – than it is for the archaeologist to date his pottery.

It is not enough to divide documents into genuine or false, or writers into trustworthy and untrustworthy, nor should one rely on a document just because, for example, it has more details than others, or is written more forcefully. These approaches, all initially useful, soon become too superficial because the average document consists of many individual statements, *each* of which may be true, untrue, partly true, ambiguous, inaccurate and so on. The critical historian, having considered the document as a whole, must move on to consider each statement, and somehow attempt to assess both its meaning and reliability. In the first place is he confident about the meaning of the statement, its language and vocabulary, its modes of thought and expression? Is the language, for example, to be taken literally or metaphorically? If there is more than one way of interpreting a statement, then the historian must make a reasoned effort to find what was intended by the writer.

Secondly, in the light of existing knowledge, is each statement likely to be true? Is it consistent internally with other statements in the same document, and externally with what other sources tell him on that subject? For example, several facts imperfectly established of themselves may combine to form a collective certainty. Furthermore, as Langlois and Seignobos expounded so well, the historian must bring into play his own experience from everyday life of the ways in which truth gets wilfully or unwittingly distorted and outright lies are propagated.[15] Is it the kind of fact that a person with known prejudices and interests, or a person concerned to put across a certain case, is likely to distort? Or conversely, is it the sort of fact that was too obvious and well-known to be distorted? Perhaps most important of all, is it likely that the writer was in a good position either to observe this fact for himself, or to acquire it from some reliable source? Thus, by systematic questioning of the nature of the fact, its context and its writer, the historian will try to assess (in terms of probability, not certain proof) the reliability of his evidence.

To show how the historian analyzes a statement and pursues the question of involvement, let us take the hypothetical example used in the first chapter: 'On May 20th 1620, the parish church was burnt down.' This is relatively straightforward, but its value as precise evidence would depend on where it was found and how it was written. Let us assume that it was found in the relevant parish register against the year 1620. The context will make it clear of course which church the statement is referring to: in other words, a single statement always has to be studied in the light of other statements in the same source, as well as in the light of different sources. If the sentence were written in apparently the same hand as the ordinary entries, the historian would be tempted to conclude that it had been written by the parson, and probably fairly soon after the event. He may even by cross-reference to other documents be able to show that this is the handwriting of, say, William Smith, who was rector of the parish from 1608 until 1623.

Conversely, the statement could be written in a hand other than that used for the normal entries. Much would then depend on whether the hand looked contemporary or later: if contemporary, it would have much the same value as the parson's; if later, one must allow for the fact that the writer has probably not based his statement on direct experience, but on some

intermediate source of information – with an increased chance
of inaccuracy and error. Of course with such an innocuous
statement it is unlikely that the writer is saying something
totally false, but he could for example have got the date wrong.
We are entitled to ask, how did he know this fact? Did he
use an earlier document contemporary with the event? Did
he meet an old inhabitant who remembered the fire? (If so,
how did the old man remember such a precise date?) Did
he use a persistent local legend? These questions should be
asked of any document or statement which does not appear
to be contemporary with the events described. For that matter,
even a so-called contemporary description must involve a
lag of time between the event and the writing, and so the same
considerations apply: we must ask ourselves whether the writer
is relying on memory, or long-hand notes, or short-hand notes,
or documents written by others. If the point were really
important, the historian would undoubtedly look for other
corroborative evidence. For example the burning of a church
may be mentioned in visitation records, ecclesiastical court
proceedings, faculties, briefs, glebe terriers (surveys of
ecclesiastical property) and so on. Even where no other
documents can be found bearing on the subject, archaeological
evidence may help; it will not provide an exact date, but it
may show that the present church was rebuilt in a style known
(by cross-reference to historical sources) to be 17th-century,
or at least that there are fire-reddened stones in the fabric.

So the same statement in different handwritings and in
different places could represent quite different levels of involvement. Some versions are almost contemporary with the events
described, and may be based on direct experience and short-
term memory; others are separated from the events by lapses
of time, and as they are not the direct record of an eye-witness,
they must be based on at least one intermediate form of written
or oral evidence. Of course involvement does not only mean
the chronological relationship between events and descriptions
it also implies the writer's *interest* in the events. Any historical
source and narrative enshrines the subjective interests, opinions
and prejudices of the writer: the historian is always on his
guard against these, and in his interpretation must allow for
their distorting effect on the truth. Was the writer himself
in any way implicated in the event? Did he write in order to
put over a particular case or argument? Does his occupation

and social status have any bearing on the attitude he took? Even an apparently straightforward statement, such as the one about the church fire, could contain distortion and prejudice, particularly of a negative kind: in a period when parish churches were often neglected, could not the parson have been somehow involved in the fire? What is the writer's attitude to the event? How much is left unsaid in this apparently simple, factual sentence?

CHRONICLES AND RECORDS

The crucial question of involvement helps us to distinguish the two main classes of document, usually known as chronicles and records.

Chronicles are historical narratives, consciously written for posterity.[16] We normally associate the term with the Middle Ages, thinking of such people as the Venerable Bede and Froissart, but they can appear at any period. For example, modern political memoirs and autobiographies are really of this genre. Often the main value of a chronicle is not so much in its account of the past, as in the highly-revealing personal record of contemporary life. This is exemplified by Matthew Paris, the greatest of all English medieval chroniclers, who knew many of the leading figures at the court of Henry III, and in 1247 was actually asked by the king to write an accurate record of the times 'lest in the future their memory be in any way lost to posterity'.[17] All this means that the chronicler must be judged as an historian, that is, as an individual who has 'processed' his evidence for posterity to read. Even the most factual accounts, which do no more than list dates, kings, battles and other events, are inevitably based on personal selection and the editing of written or oral sources. If he is an intelligent observer of contemporary life and seeks reliable evidence for other events, then a chronicler provides valuable information which may not be recoverable in other ways – a fact which, since the 19th and early 20th centuries when so many chronicles were edited and published, we tend to overlook in our current preoccupation with records.

The second category of documents, records, were originally produced as part of everyday life and work, mainly for the use of contemporaries. Very often they are the products of business and administration – good examples are minute-books, accounts, rentals and surveys. Or they can be rather more domestic in nature, like certain receipts for bread and beer which, being contemporary with the great temples of Uruk dating to the mid-fourth millennium BC, are among the earliest documents in human history to survive. Because they were primarily compiled for contemporary use, records have no conscious historical purpose. This does not mean that they always tell the truth, nor that they have no personal bias and opinion. It does however mean that the writer's involvement with his material is of a totally different order from the chronicler's, and that his predominantly contemporary purposes give the historians a more direct (or perhaps less indirect) insight into the life of the past. As historical evidence, records are largely unconscious, and not slanted for the consumption of posterity. In this they are therefore akin to the vast majority of archaeological artifacts.[18]

There are two other important observations which must be made about records. In the first place, it is not true to say that they have absolutely *no* concern with posterity. As the word implies, records once written were intended to be kept and bequeathed to future generations. Important decisions had to be registered, and ownership and rights defined, so that if any dispute arose the record could be consulted. For example, an enclosure award was a legal document which laid down for contemporaries the details of an immensely complicated rearrangement of property and rights, but it was also meant to be the basis of a new order stretching into the future: the award remains a highly important legal document today and is often consulted. Strictly therefore, a record is concerned with the future, but in a legalistic rather than an historical sense.

Secondly, it would be a mistake to regard records as heaps of ready-made facts. Although they contain relatively straightforward statements, they also contain judgements, opinions, interests and prejudices – and these can colour even mundane documents like accounts and title-deeds. In other words they, like chronicles, contain a subjective element which must be allowed for by the historian. However, the subjective element in records is at least contemporaneous with the events it describes, and therefore constitutes in itself interesting and original historical evidence.

Kitson Clark has recently demonstrated with great clarity how apparently sober and straightforward records can mislead

historians.[19] Various kinds of minute-book, he points out,
are an attempt to record speeches, discussions and arguments
– especially in organized and formal gatherings such as com-
mittees, courts and enquiries. Much that purports to be a
direct record of speech, or is used with the convention of inverted
commas, is in fact reconstructed *after* the event. Most minute-
books for example are written up hours or days after the
meeting, on the basis of scribbled or shorthand notes taken at
the time. The difference between the original rough minutes
and the 'fair copy' can be considerable. Any record of this
kind is a personal summary of what the writer thought was
significant and worthy of mention, both at the time and later;
he rejected what he thought was insignificant.

Although the majority of records and chronicles are in
manuscript in their original form, it must be remembered that
ever since the invention of the printing-press some evidence
has been in printed form. For example newspapers are an
important source in modern history, and are in essence latter-
day chronicles. Many a government report, a vital kind of
record, is only obtainable in print. Because printing is a
technique for making multiple copies, the physical or archaeological character of such a source differs somewhat from that of
a manuscript (which is essentially unique). A printed document
should always be regarded as a fair copy of an earlier manuscript (or typescript) version, though of course the latter
only rarely survives.

It is obvious then that there is no such thing as a self-evident
historical fact, which the historian simply has to read to understand. The historian has no means of knowing the past save
through his documentary evidence, and this is essentially
personal and indirect. The so-called 'facts' of history are
innumerable statements about events, places, dates, personalities
and attitudes. Often there is no dispute about them, especially
when there is plenty of corroborating evidence. But they nevertheless differ from an interpretative judgement only in their
degree of complexity: a 'fact' is only a less complicated statement of opinion. E. H. Dance has summed this up memorably
by pointing out that such a familiar statement of 'fact' as
'Battle of Hastings, AD 1066' contains at least two mis-state-
ments of fact and one expression of religious prejudice! The
battle was not fought at Hastings but at Senlac, six or seven
miles away; Christ was not born in the 31st year of Augustus'

reign, so the date is actually wrong; the religious prejudice comes of imposing Christian chronology on a largely non-Christian world.[20] Of course, one could say that these are amusing philosophical quibbles, but they do make the essential point that apparently simple facts are as much processed, reconstructed and interpreted as are the more elaborate patterns of cause and effect.

E. H. Carr has made an interesting distinction between 'facts about the past' and true 'historical facts'.[21] To him a fact is only historical when it has been used in an interpretation; unless a fact has been used by an historian, it remains a 'fact about the past'. This is primarily a matter of personal definition, but it is important to stress that there is undoubtedly an historical thesis that will make every true fact significant (i.e. meaningful, not necessarily important). The selection of facts is not just sorting significant information from insignificant; it is the finding of facts that are relevant to the subject and its interpretation. There is therefore no historical fact which is totally insignificant – every fact has significance in a certain context. The example used by Carr concerns a seller of gingerbread at Stalybridge Wakes in 1850, who was kicked to death by an angry mob. Such a fact may not seem very significant to a political historian, but it could be of interest and even importance to an historian concerned with social conditions, or law and order, or markets and fairs, or simply the local history of Stalybridge. J. Renier has put this well by saying that 'one historian's occurrence is another's event.'[22]

One of the most important results of comparing sources is the ability to distinguish 'common form'. Many documents, particularly those which were legal and administrative in purpose, have a standard plan, and use set expressions and formulae. On first reading a borough charter for instance, one needs to know what a 'gild-merchant' and 'free burgage' are, how common or rare such charters are, the reigns in which they were issued, and so on. These problems are especially associated with the records of offical bodies, such as government departments and courts of law, and they can only be solved by a study of the appropriate administrative machinery and the classes of document which it issued. One of the most common historical mistakes is the acceptance of common form as specific information, and sometimes *vice versa*. Most documents will contain both elements, and it is the historian's task to distinguish them.[23]

The work of the documentary historian, like that of the archaeologist, is steadily becoming more mathematical and statistical: indeed the word *cliometrics* has already been coined to describe the development! Where the evidence allows, it must surely be admitted that numbers are more precise vehicles of historical meaning than commonplace words which do no more than *imply* quantification (e.g., more, less, possibly, probably, nearly, almost, etc.). Furthermore there are many historical sources which either use figures directly (such as accounts and rentals) or give long lists of detail crying out for quantification (such as parish registers and censuses). An historian's conclusions too, on subjects such as demography and occupation-structure, may be best expressed and summarized in numbers and diagrams. Obviously such methods could run riot, and nobody relishes history produced entirely by means of punched cards, graphs, tables and computers; but providing the result is greater precision and concision, numerical analysis must increasingly play its part in the study of history.[24]

The historian cannot squeeze a document dry without systematically organizing the information it yields. Therefore, having given considerable thought to the precise meaning of the words involved, he must construct (either mentally or on paper) a connected series of detailed and penetrating questions which are designed to sort out the statements. Although they will have interpretative assumptions built into them, the questions enable the historian to organize the data verbally and numerically, and lead to the refinement of a number of fact-judgements. A sample of such an analytical scheme, for late-17th-century Hearth Tax returns, is given in the table opposite: it contains several interpretative assumptions, for example that names bracketed together in the returns represent tenements within the same buildings.

SYNTHESIS

The interpretation of individual statements produces the tested facts necessary for historical writing, but, in the words of W.G. Hoskins, these are 'the uncooked potatoes and not the finished meal'.[25] There still remains the final creative task of synthesizing the disparate facts into a piece of original historical reconstruction, and of expressing this reconstruction in clear,

HEARTH TAX RETURNS – A SCHEME FOR ANALYSIS

---

1 Number of tax-paying households?

2 Number of exempt households?

3 Total number of households?

4 Estimated total population? (Multiplier, 4.5)

5 Number of people with social status indicated? List them with details (e.g. *Mr* Girlinge, John Bedingfield *Esq.*)

6 Number of women? Number of widows specified?

7 Number of separate houses? (Omit empty houses and tenements)

8 Number of *groups* of tenements   *a*   for 2 households?
                                        b   for 3 households?
                                        c   for more than 3 households?

9 Number of *individual* tenements? (List payers and non-payers separately)

10 Empty houses

11 Total number of dwelling units (houses and individual tenements)

12 Check total number of hearths

13 Sizes of houses (including groups of tenements).
   How many with   1   hearth?
      ,,   ,,   ,,   2   hearths?
      ,,   ,,   ,,   3   ,,
      ,,   ,,   ,,   4   ,,
      ,,   ,,   ,,   5 – 7   ,,
      ,,   ,,   ,,   8 – 10 ,,
      ,,   ,,   ,,   11 – 15 ,,
      ,,   ,,   ,,   16 – 20 ,,
      ,,   ,,   ,,   21 –   ,,

14 Sizes of individual tenements.   How many with 1 hearth?
                                                       How many with 2 hearths?
                                                     How many with 3 hearths?

15 Any other information? (Almshouses, workhouses, town-houses, effects of fires)

NOTE Where one reads entries like 'Poore. That receive collection 15', one can assume that the number refers to *hearths*. To get the minimum number of households that such a figure represents, one should divide by 2, because this is the maximum number of hearths which the poor usually have (round *up* fractions to nearest whole number). The result is probably an underestimate, but it is always better to record minimum figures.

humane language. Three distinct processes are involved, all interpretative by nature.

Having decided what aspects of his subject he is going to concentrate on, and the order in which he wishes to treat them, the historian will firstly sort, group and cross-reference his facts – to make sure that like is associated with like, and that all possible causal relationships between facts are considered. The classification is of course usually by some combination of subject, period, locality and persons. Secondly, the historian will attempt to create, by logic or numerical calculation, totally new facts which help to fill in some of the gaps in the record and which illustrate the significance of his original information. For example, by studying the individual entries of a parish register, a local historian may be able to show that in a certain year one-fifth of the population died – yet nowhere in original sources did he read that statement. This is a new fact, partly verbal, partly numerical; it generalizes at a higher level many different, particularizing statements in the register.

Lastly, the historian will construct in his mind a final, overall interpretation of the subject, which though it is his personal view of the past, will inevitably contain ideas derived from the work of other historians. It is an attempt to see shape and pattern in a mass of detail and to sort out significant events from the less significant – according, that is, to the argument being presented. In this final synthesis facts of many different kinds will be welded together: some will be simple, particular events (such as a date of birth, or the itinerary of a journey); some will be of a much more generalized kind (such as the expectation of life, or the standard of living at a particular period); others will involve complex, psychological considerations (concerning, for example, the character and motives of individuals). At this stage many facts which were laboriously won, turn out to be inessential to the argument being presented, and are therefore rejected.

The new mathematical history at its most advanced may be able to calculate how important certain factors were in a given historical situation, and even what *might* have happened if one variable had been different. This could obviously be of great value in any historical synthesis. The classic example is R. W. Fogel's work on the effect of the railways on American economic growth in the 19th century.[26] But this sort of numerical interpretation will only be possible within very strict limits (where, for example, the documentation is complete, and the number of potential variables is small), and it is no more proven than the more normal verbal judgements of history.

To equip him for his task, the historian must have two attributes above all. First, he must be rational, and subject his evidence at every stage to cool, critical and analytical reasoning. In an historical situation, everything must have a rational explanation – even when human beings have behaved in a most irrational or insane manner. The second element in the historian's mental equipment is imagination. Because of the necessarily incomplete and indirect nature of documentary evidence, the historian often has to judge for himself the true relationship between events, and what people's real thoughts or motives were. Imagination here does not mean wild speculation; it must be carefully rooted in the evidence which does exist, and controlled by learning and experience. A deep understanding of, and sympathy for, the period is clearly a vital part of the process.

So how does the final interpretation of the historian emerge? As he begins to get the measure of his subject, he will pay particular attention to the judgements and opinions that have been expressed about it, whether by contemporaries, chroniclers or earlier historians. In the light of old and new evidence, he will be slowly impelled to accept some judgements, but to doubt others. Gradually a new interpretation will form in his mind. This may in turn cause him to think of, and find, new sources of information, which may confirm the interpretation but more likely cause it to be modified. There is therefore a constant interaction at all times and at all levels between the basic information and the emergent hypothesis. The historian does not turn to interpretation at the last moment, after all the earlier steps in research have been carried out: no sooner has he thought about a subject for research than he embarks on a process of continuous interpretation and re-interpretation. It is a laborious and painful process which involves the examination of countless ideas, the acceptance of some and the rejection of the majority, until eventually the stage is reached where the interpretation seems to fit all available and relevant facts, where no more significant facts can be found, and where no inconvenient facts have been suppressed. The final result of the historical process is an original and personal account of what happened in the past. It involves the imposition of a personal argument or pattern on the disparate evidence, in the belief that this corresponds most closely to the complicated truth. In the last analysis, therefore, historical truth is not proved: after much study and thought the historian erects a thesis or reconstruction which he believes and argues is *probably* true.

4 The relationship between archaeology and history

After an analysis of their individual methods, it is worth discussing the relationship between archaeology and history, and in so far as it can be separated, the relationship between the two professions, in order to see how far co-operation and true integration are possible.

The first obvious similarity between the two subjects is that the students of each attempt to write history in the broad sense, that is, they are trying to reconstruct as fully and accurately as possible the story of human life in the past. The archaeologist no less than the historian, is, in Wheeler's telling words, 'not digging up things, he is digging up people; however much he may analyse and dessicate his discussions in the laboratory, the ultimate appeal across the ages . . . is from mind to intelligent mind, from man to sentient man'.[1] It is worth remembering also that the final product in both disciplines is a written account – an historical reconstruction of the past in the form of written statements – which immediately becomes an historical document in its own right, to be studied critically like any other kind of berbal evidence.

Both archaeology and history suffer from the fact that their evidence is woefully incomplete. The archaeologist is usually able to study those cultural relics which are hard and relatively imperishable, such as pottery, flint and bronze. Only very rarely do softer materials survive, such as cloth, rope, basketry, wood, meat and leather, yet these and others must have been very important in the 'equipment' of so many societies. Occasional freak finds such as the clothing, felt hangings, carpets and tattooed bodies of Pazyryk (U.S.S.R.), the wooden figures at the source of the River Seine and the uncorrupted flesh of the Tollund man are exceptions which make us realize how much is usually lost. Much of the archaeologist's precious technological and economic evidence has therefore decayed, and he must always make some allowance for things which have not survived, or at least have not been recognized. Of course improved excavation techniques have resulted in the discovery of evidence which would have been overlooked by earlier generations, and doubtless new scientific techniques will enable future excavators to find things which are overlooked today. Nevertheless there will always be a considerable amount which it is not physically or economically possible to recover, or which has perished without trace.

As time goes on, the problems connected with the survival and recovery of evidence become more acute. In fact archaeology today faces an unprecedented crisis. Not only is excavation necessarily slower and more painstaking than it was, but all over the world the pace at which sites are being destroyed and chance finds made, is accelerating rapidly. This means that much energy and great resources are being diverted from proper planned campaigns of research, designed to solve specific problems, into digging sites simply because they exist and are threatened.

Similarly a vast amount of documentary evidence has been, and is being, destroyed, and the historian has to make do with what is left. In this field too the accidents of survival and recovery operate. Some documents seem to survive entirely by accident, but many were kept deliberately as a record by individuals and institutions in such places as parish chests, solicitors' offices, courts of law and government departments. Countless documents await discovery in the sense that they are forgotten, misplaced and lost. Many of these are in private hands or, if in a repository, are not catalogued or listed. At all periods, masses of written documents have been deliberately destroyed or kept so badly that they have rotted away.

Perhaps destruction is not such a serious problem for the contemporary historian as it is for the archaeologist. Record offices and libraries increasingly encourage the public to deposit or register documents and, provided they are kept from destruction, they do not have to be worked upon immediately. Furthermore, techniques such as microfilming mean that, if necessary facsimiles can be made. Nevertheless, whereas the archaeologist has some idea of the amount of destruction going on (through aerial photography, the recovery of some artifacts, and the amount of urban and rural development), the historian is completely in the dark – if documents are unregistered, they are totally unknown.

Even if all the documents and other physical objects of the past had survived, there would still be events in human history that left no traces and which would therefore be irrecoverable. Many an important conversation and decision, for example, was never recorded in any way. There can therefore never be anything approaching a complete history. The history that is written is determined by the evidence which survives, and by the interest which we as historians take in what survives.

It is also worth repeating here another similarity between history and archaeology which has already been mentioned. In neither case is the specialist simply presented with the historical truth; both kinds of evidence have to be carefully processed and interpreted by people who fully understand the potentialities inherent in each. Archaeologists must carefully probe for the thought-processes which lie behind physical objects, while historians must critically examine statements in an attempt to find their true significance. In each case the final interpretation is a personal reconstruction which is only probabilistic in nature and not capable of final proof. The past cannot be re-lived nor can the vast majority of its characters be met and questioned, but at least it can be partially reconstructed by the skilled study of present traces.

In the first chapter it was argued that the essential difference between history and archaeology lies in their respective raw materials – statements on the one hand and physical objects on the other. From this, other differences inevitably flow. The critical analysis and interpretation of statements which, as we have already argued, both historians and archaeologists engage in, is entirely an internal, intellectual process. By contrast, when an archaeologist or historian turns to physical objects, he must assess them visually. A blind man could never be a successful student of material remains, however acute his sense of touch, because sight is the most immediate means of studying the evidence. However, a blind man could be a successful interpreter of statements: he would of course miss most of the archaeological information latent in the document as a physical object, but providing somebody could read the sources to him (and it makes no differences essentially whether a statement is read or heard) he could carry out the basic intellectual analysis and reconstruction which owes nothing to sight.

Another very important difference concerns the effect study has on the raw materials. Excavation is not the only means of

obtaining archaeological information but it is the most important. As a site is excavated, so is it destroyed. 'From the moment
when an archaeological excavator lifts the first shovelful of earth
he has begun a process of destruction for which the only com-
pensation is complete and immediate record'.[2] The superimposed
structures are revealed and the artifacts raised, while the vital
stratification is being stripped away. The artifacts themselves,
including some monuments, wholly survive, but the stratification only survives in so far as it was correctly dug, observed,
and recorded during the excavation. One consequence of this
destruction is that excavation has to be done carefully so that
no two layers are confused, and everything recorded so that
each object has a context. If a mistake is made in the excavation
or recording, it is irreparable. The archaeologist therefore has
a great moral responsibility to dig and record to the highest
possible standards, because nobody can subsequently revise
his original work. By contrast an historian does not destroy
his evidence as he proceeds; if he does make a mistake in, say,
transcribing a document, it is technically possible for a later
scholar to correct it. For example Cardinal Gasquet's edition
of Premonstratensian documents has called forth at least three
lists of corrections from other scholars.[3] The historical equivalent of the archaeological situation would be for the historian
to burn his manuscript after working on it!

It has often been said that archaeological evidence is 'unconscious'. By this we mean that human beings in the past did
not for the most part leave behind their physical remains as
deliberate historical evidence, whereas some at least of the
historians's documents, such as chronicles, biographies, memoirs
and diaries, were clearly meant for posterity to read and use.
Archaeological evidence is generally much more of an historical
accident. Though an artifact can survive for thousands of years,
it was made to meet an immediate need, and not for the benefit
of future generations. The same can be said for, say, domestic
houses or field-systems; these were intended to last for years,
and often in fact survived in use for more than one lifetime, but
like artifacts they were functional and not constructed with
posterity in mind.

Nevertheless it is not entirely true to say that *all* archaeological
evidence is unconscious, and that the desire or at least the vague
hope of impressing posterity was *never* present. Surely the makers
of beautiful objects like a jadeite axe, or still more the builders

of a great monument like Karnak, conceived the possibility that their creations, on which they had expended thought and love, would survive into the future and be appreciated by generations to come – even though the immediate purpose was probably to impress contemporaries, or as an offering to a deity. There is no doubt that the great medieval cathedrals and Renaissance paintings were partly at least meant for posterity; why should we doubt that this motive could at times be present in the minds of people, whose achievements were more modest? But in spite of this important qualification, there is no doubt that the majority of artifacts and other kinds of archaeological evidence are an 'historical accident, less loaded than a document with the desire to inform and impress'.[4] The table below (after R.T. Shafer and John Vincent) classifies types of consciously and unconsciously transmitted historical evidence.

I *Consciously transmitted*

    a Written: annals, chronicles, some inscriptions, diaries, memoirs, genealogies

    b Oral
       1 Traditional: ballads, tales, sagas
       2 Contemporary interviews

    c Art works: historical paintings and mosaics, portraits, scenic sculpture, coins, medals, some films

II *Unconsciously transmitted*

    a Human remains

    b Written 'mere' records (e.g., business, military, government)

    c Oral: e.g., wiretapped conversation

    d Language

    e Customs and institutions

    f Artifacts
       1 Artistic works
       2 Tools, etc.

It is also said that whereas history deals with personalities, archaeology is impersonal. It is certainly true that historical evidence deals *inter alia* with individuals, their personalities and biographical details; it also brings us into direct contact with the specific personal thought of people from the past. The archaeologist uses material which, though the result or expression of thought, is not explicit. His physical objects proclaim themselves as products of human workmanship, and sometimes possess great beauty and individuality, but they can tell us very little about their makers' personalities, beliefs and life story.

Archaeological evidence certainly does not trade in names and personalities but it is not accurate to describe it as utterly impersonal. To handle the pottery, tools and weapons of long-dead people is partially to resurrect them and to conjure up a vision of everyday life. To some extent human beings do express their personalities in the choice of objects with which they surround themselves, as well as in their thoughts, beliefs and writings. Imagine entering a room or house belonging to someone you have never met and know nothing about. From physical objects alone, you will not be able to name the owner, to judge his intelligence and temperament, or to assess to any depth his political and religious beliefs. But you may conclude that he is a person of considerable wealth and taste, who reads books (even though he may not understand them) and enjoys food and drink, who uses a wheel-chair, smokes cigars and plays darts. These things by themselves by no means amount to a complete personality, and could apply to many different people, but they are not impersonal. Because archaeological evidence is anonymous, it is not *ipso facto* impersonal. As E. H. Carr has said, 'people do not cease to be people, or individuals individuals, because we do not know their names.'[5]

In spite of the interesting glimpses which archaeology occasionally affords us of human individuals, in the main the archaeologist is forced to ignore the part 'played by the will, the decision, even the caprice, of dominant personalities'.[6] Dominant personalities may well have shaped some of the archaeological record before us, but the evidence is either too fragmentary or too vague and ambiguous for us to recognize it in such terms. For example, if by some fortunate accident an archaeologist were to find the site where some gifted individual had discovered the technique of metal-working, he would not recognize it as such. It would go into the record as the earliest-known site of its kind. This individual and his unique distinction could only, in fact, be recorded in documentary evidence.

Archaeological evidence is therefore mainly confined to the study of groups, whereas the documentary historian can study both individuals *and* groups (and their interaction). In the past century or so, historians have increasingly developed their interest in social groups. At first it was economic historians who led the way. For example, T.S. Ashton wrote that the subject matter of economic history 'is not Adam, a gardener, but the cultivators of the soil as a class; not Tubal-Cain, a skilled artificer in brass and iron, but metal workers or industrialists in general.'[7] Social historians, under the influence of modern 'sociology, have carried further this interest in the relationship between individuals and the society of which they form part. Conversely sociologists have increasingly realized the importance of the past in the shaping of society, and are themselves beginning to use historical sources and methods. This development is a salutary one in several respects, not least because by increasingly using sociological and economic concepts historians will become more aware of the very similar approach of the archaeologist. Various branches of social science, including archaeology, are concerned with communities, groups, societies and cultures, and they place considerable emphasis on classification and the comparative method.

Again, it is often said with a great deal of truth that archaeology deals with 'states' and history with 'events'. States are the relatively static or slow-moving conditions of life; they are the broad long-term background involving such things as technical equipment, basic economy and standards of living. Against this background, events take place – battles and war, famine and plenty, the enactment of laws, the rise and fall of leaders, public scandals, and triumphs. In the archaeological record there may well be traces of events, but the extent to which the archaeologist can reconstruct them is strictly limited compared with the opportunities presented to the historian. Think of the great war-cemetery at Maiden Castle in Dorset: here is *par excellence* an example of an event in the archaeological record.[8] Thirty-eight skeletons were found in the eastern entrance of the hill-fort, in rough irregular graves cut into the ruins of buildings and a layer of ash. The skeletons had been thrown into the graves in all manner of attitudes and represented men and women, young and old. In ten cases the skulls showed extensive cuts, and in one famous skeleton a Roman ballista-bolt was found embedded in the vertebrae. The victims were 'Belgicized' British natives, and the victors Roman troops. But the more one knows, the more one needs to know, and here archaeology begins to fail us. Who was the British commander? Did he

exhort his defenders to supreme efforts, perhaps in the way
that the near-contemporary Eleazar Ben Ya'ir is said to have
harangued the Zealot defenders of Masada beside the Dead
Sea?[9] (Documentary evidence of course suggests that Vespasian
was likely to have been the Roman commander). How long did
the battle last? What tactics did each side adopt? How many
defenders and attackers were there? What were the political
and military results of the victory?

Events, then, will leave traces in the archaeological record,
especially those which had some obvious effect on the physical
environment (such as battles, volcanic eruptions, earthquakes
and fires), but we shall rarely find more than a general outline,
and the finer details will have to be supplied, if at all, by documents. The vast majority of the decisive events of human history
have probably left no trace whatsoever in the physical record, or
at least no trace which can be interpreted in significant-enough
terms.

Another aspect of the same problem is that archaeology
and history have rather different time-scales. The historian is
commonly concerned with relatively short periods of time,
and can work quite satisfactorily within the age-span of a single
individual or generation. Richard Atkinson has pointed out
that 'whatever the deficiencies of the actual evidence it is surely
true that the ultimate aim of the interpreter of history is to
study the reactions of men to the situations in which they found
themselves *within their own lifetime*'.[10] This is undoubtedly
true, though of course many historians do concern themselves
with longer spans of time involving many individuals and
generations. The archaeologist by contrast is hardly ever able
to find evidence which makes sense in terms of a single human life;
his evidence is much cruder and only begins to have significance
in terms of the life of a total society or community, usually
over a long period of time. Even when dating methods are much
more refined than they are today, we shall never do more than
catch the occasional glimpse of the human individual and his
brief span on earth.

In general one could perhaps regard archaeological time as
falling between the finely-detailed time-scale of the historian
and the crude immensities of geological and astronomical time,
but recent developments have high-lighted interesting variations
within archaeological time itself. Archaeology certainly covers
more of the human past than does documentary history: for

all its crudity and ambiguity prehistory has the special distinction of perspectives which are longer than any other form of human history. However, archaeology is not for ever committed to the long perspectives only, fascinating though these are historically and philosophically. The importance of studying the archaeology of more recent documented periods is partly that co-ordination with historical statements gives a far more detailed, truly absolute time-scale than prehistory will ever achieve in its 'text-free' innocence.

Compared with the majority of archaeologists, documentary historians find it easier to accept that history comes right down to the present. To use Kitson Clark's words, 'history is the record of what has happened in the past, of anything that has ever happened in the past, however long ago or however recently . . . . It is better to accept, as an axiom, the definition that any attempt to describe what has happened before the actual moment of narration shall be called history.'[11] Of course there are practical difficulties – for example the sheer quantity of some kinds of evidence, and the total inaccessibility of other kinds – and these have admittedly caused some historians to draw the line at some arbitrary date such as 1914 or 1939.

Given that history has a much better chance of revealing the individual, there does seem to be a genuine difference between the range of social groups within a society that are revealed by archaeology and history respectively. Because the finding of archaeological evidence is basically a gamble (by the accidents of survival and discovery) and because all social groups use physical objects, archaeology is capable of finding evidence from all orders of society. A rich and powerful man is likely to have had more possessions than a poor man, and this may mean that the record is to some extent biased socially. For example Bronze Age round barrows may well have been raised by relatively affluent people, whereas the lower orders were buried in flat graves which will generally be found only by accident. Nevertheless both rich and poor at all periods did have material equipment in the shape of various artifacts and monuments. There are many sites which give us some idea of the standard of life among the great mass of the population. Indeed it often seems a basic assumption by excavators that the sites are typical: that Star Carr for instance is no Mesolithic palace, but an ordinary settlement of the Maglemosean culture of the 8th millennium BC. One of the peculiar fascinations of archaeology is that it sheds light on the lives of the submerged majority as well as on ruling minorities. The archaeologist 'must be concerned with the lives and achievements of countless ordinary, anonymous people'.[12]

Historical evidence is rather different. It is the written record left behind by certain distinct elements in society, who are likely to be a small minority. Let us take as an example the documents, which survive from the Middle Ages in Britain. These are likely to be either quite deliberate historical accounts by chroniclers, or records of a strongly legalistic and administrative nature. In the main they are the compilations of administrators at various levels, lawyers and above all, ecclesiastics – in short, a tiny minority of educated and literate people. The great mass of the population did not leave anything in the way of a personal record, nor are they mentioned by the literate except as cogs in the machinery of local government and national taxation. The medieval peasant farmer in an obscure village may feature in the court rolls of his manor (when he took up his tenement or committed various misdemeanours), or as a name in an Exchequer list, but only very rarely do we find enough evidence to assess a man's life and personality. This is why the excavation of peasants' houses, and the finding of their pottery and other artifacts, adds such an important new dimension to the study of the period.

Even in more modern times it is often extremely difficult to find evidence for the personal lives of the masses. For example in England the 19th-century villagers and industrial workers are only slightly less elusive than medieval peasants. It is significant that their examination as paupers before a magistrate may provide the best opportunity we have of studying their lives. Where diaries or biographies survive, they are likely to describe rather exceptional individuals like trade-union leaders, evangelists and criminals. Even today, when most of the population is literate, and the output of printed, typescript and manuscript material is enormous, very little is kept which will provide a personal record of the vast majority of people. Huge quantities of documents are regarded as ephemeral and are destroyed. Only exceptional people with one eye cocked on posterity are, for instance, likely to keep personal correspondence; the majority only keep important legal documents such as insurance policies, mortgage agreements, title-deeds, birth certificates and so on. To be of use to the historian, records have not only to be made, but also to be kept.[13] All this adds up to the fact that documentary evidence tends to comprise the records of the governing classes, or of exceptionally able and determined individuals. This is why the mainstream of historical studies has always been, and always will be, concerned with political, legal and constitutional affairs.

Is it true, as some would say, that archaeological evidence is inferior to historical? This is an extraordinarily difficult question to answer; it has been debated for centuries and is wide open to special pleading. Of course the whole argument depends on how one defines superiority and inferiority. In one sense, because archaeological evidence is less 'conscious' and less liable therefore to deceive, it can be said to be superior, but there are undoubtedly two important senses in which it must be regarded as inferior. First, it is less direct evidence of human thought than an historical statement: it introduces another stage between the student and the original thought he is after. Instead of directly studying statements, the written thoughts of human beings in the past, the archaeologist studies objects on which human thought has been expended. Whereas the historical statement is explicit, the thought lying behind an artifact is implicit and unformed, and it can only be reconstructed in outline. Secondly, archaeological evidence generally concerns basic human achievements in the fields of technology and economics. It deals with the foundations of human life, more than with the superstructure of intellectual and spiritual achievement. By contrast historical evidence can illuminate both the foundations *and* the superstructure; it has a much greater coverage of the full range of human activities.

To be absolutely fair to archaeology, it should not be forgotten that its evidence includes physical works of art, and that it has adumbrated intellectual achievements of the highest order – such as the development of language and writing, and the invention of farming and metallurgy. Nor should we forget that more and more historians are choosing to study the economies and technologies of past societies, precisely the things which generally interest the archaeologist.

However, though archaeological evidence is more limited *per se,* without it there would be no such thing as verbal evidence. Elton warns us not to 'fall victim to the pleasures of the physical and visible object', yet it is precisely the much-despised object (of paper, parchment or vellum) which gives him his evidence in the first place.[14] More important than any discussion of superiority or inferiority is the recognition that although the two kinds of evidence are definably different, they are at the same time complementary and physically indissoluble.

THE TWO PROFESSIONS

Degree syllabuses are a good measure of how far the historian and the archaeologist are separately trained, and how far mutual interest, co-operation and integration are encouraged.

In British universities the vast majority of historians undergo three years of study, with the main emphasis understandably on political, constitutional and legal history. Gradually other aspects are being introduced. Economic history, developed since the late 19th century, is commonplace, but only a certain amount of social history is admitted. Occasionally, regional and local history are possible options. There is also an increasing concern with non-European continents such as Africa and South America. A minority of historians take subsidiary papers in aspects of archaeology – such as Roman Britain or Deserted Medieval Villages – and thereby acquire some knowledge of the raw materials and methods of the other subject. A few of them develop their interest in archaeology further, and concentrate as much on physical evidence as on written documents; obviously they are the most likely people to practise, or at least attempt, co-ordination.

It has already been remarked that history syllabuses in Britain contain little instruction on methods and sources. Only occasionally does one find a course offered, for example, on 'historical evidence and the nature of historical enquiry' including 'elements of archaeology'. In fact, when the syllabuses of 35 British universities were analyzed in 1966, it was found that only eleven offered courses on historical method, of which seven were compulsory. Five offered courses on palaeography (all optional). It is noticeable that these practical courses were mainly offered by the younger universities and departments.[15]

Generally, syllabuses consist of a wide range of periods, topics and 'problems' – such as British History to 1939, European History 1500-1815, the Reform of the Papacy 1046-99, and the Origins of the Second World War. In other words the emphasis is mainly on history as a body of knowledge, and as a continuing debate among historians. To be fair, there is usually a special subject in the third year, which is a more intensive study of a limited historical theme, designed to give students some familiarity with sources and their interpretation. These sources are in the vast majority of cases in printed form, so that the earlier steps in historical method are necessarily omitted, but a much more serious criticism is that this kind of instruction comes so late in the course: instead of introducing the basic methods of the subject at the beginning, and then making it relevant throughout to the great body of knowledge being surveyed, it is added almost as an afterthought. One of the most encouraging developments of recent years has been the foundation course of the Open University, which right from the start emphasizes history as a craft, and discusses the nature of historical evidence, the character of documents, palaeography, diplomatic, secondary sources, and so on.[16]

Archaeologists in the past were usually people who came to the subject after a training in some other discipline such as classics, history or geography. They were individuals who accidentally or deliberately made contact with archaeology, and were attracted to it. Often their varied backgrounds and training made them all the more effective as archaeologists, as they brought a breadth and vision which is often lacking in a single specialist training. Now, however, increasing numbers of archaeologists are being specially trained, as the number of university departments and lecturers rises. In Britain there are now several places where one can read for a degree in archaeology, either on its own or with a related subject such as history, classics or anthropology. There is little doubt that because most students of archaeology wish to practise it (either as a full-time profession or as a part-time interest) there is a much greater emphasis on methodology than for historians. They are taught such rudiments as the principles of excavation, typological classification, and various kinds of scientific and statistical analysis. The undergraduate reading archaeology today usually has a healthy awareness not only of current work and problems, but also of the actual research methods and techniques employed. There is therefore far less of a gulf between undergraduate and postgraduate work than in the field of history. Yet, little thought is given to the full chronological range of physical evidence, and to its relationship with written statements.

So, in Britain at least, the majority of historians and archaeologists are separately trained, and have infrequent contact.

This inevitably means that they remain ignorant and even suspicious of each other. To a certain extent methods are being taught, but this is usually done in far too narrow and restricting a way. Where indeed co-operation and co-ordination are practised, they are usually the result of the enthusiasm and persistence of individuals, who realize that for a particular subject or problem they must use objects and statements and weld them together into a single historical interpretation. At the moment this is happening more in spite of a person's training than because of it.

CRITICISMS DIRECTED AT ARCHAEOLOGY

The average historian knows little about archaeology, but this does not prevent him from making criticisms of it. These are worth considering, because like all prejudices they usually contain a grain of truth. An historian will sometimes object to the lack of historical interpretation in archaeological literature. After reading long lists of finds, and an account of the stratification and structures on a site, he will quite legitimately ask, so what? What does it all add up to historically? Who actually lived there, for how long, what was their way of life, why was the place abandoned?

In the face of this criticism, one must freely admit that too often the historical interpretation of an excavation is buried in a welter of detail, or is missing altogether. Whatever the amount of descriptive and analytical material in an archaeological report, there must always be an overall historical interpretation which attempts to extract the essential human significance of the project, and to express it in clear, jargon-free language. Contrary to what some archaeologists think, this does not mean incautiously talking of possibilities and probabilities as certainties: it means, as it does for the documentary historian, the clearest expression of probabilistic judgements. The long lists of finds and other details in an excavation report must not be regarded as ends in themselves: only as the cumbersome apparatus for distilling a few, precious, historical statements.

Of course critics should realize that, by the nature of the subject, archaeological reports have to be long, detailed and costly. This is the result, first, of the amount of cultural material to be studied, and secondly, of the destructive nature of excavation. The vital stratigraphic evidence exists only in so far as it was correctly recorded: hence the many lists and appendices. All this must be intensely irritating to the historian who is competing for space in a national or local journal – all he has to do is to give simple quotations from, and references to, his sources.

Nevertheless, it is surely true that archaeologists need to give more thought to what is worthy of publication. Far too much basically descriptive material is printed which ought not to take up space in journals, but should be stored in manuscript or typescript form in museums, or at the very most be cyclostyled. At present it is far too easy to publish archaeological reports which have little or no historical content. One thinks for instance of those rag-bag lists of new finds in county journals – a scatter of pottery here, or a coin there. Both the material and a description of its finding should be lodged with the local museum, where interested people can find them. In other words, it should be a recognized function of the modern museum to store archives as well as the normal range of material things.[17]

Archaeologists rightly seize on any method which will wring more information from physical objects. This inevitably means the increasing use of techniques borrowed from the physical, natural and social sciences. As more technical detail emerges, so reports get longer. This worries many critics, particularly those who belong to the older 'historical' school of archaeology. For example, Jacquetta Hawkes has recently given a strong warning against the dangers of 'scientific' archaeology: to her some publications are 'so esoteric, so overburdened with unhelpful jargon, so grossly inflated in relation to the significance of the matters involved, that they might emanate from a secret society, an introverted group of specialists enjoying their often rather squalid intellectual spells and rituals at the expense of an outside world to which they will contribute nothing that is enjoyable, generally interesting or of historical importance'.[18] This is powerful stuff, and the basic complaint that the historical and human purposes of archaeology are being forgotten is undoubtedly justified. But in another sense the criticism is unfair, because it is the job of the archaeologist to observe and record *minutiae* in the hope that they turn out, either immediately or at a later date, to be significant historically. One simply cannot always tell whether a fact is, or is not, of value. As an excavation proceeds, the director is constantly making decisions and judgements, but where he is uncertain of the value of a detail, it is

incumbent on him to record it – in the hope that its real significance will be appreciated later.

The same writer criticized Charles McBurney's mammoth
report on Haua Fteah, a Palaeolithic cave in Cyrenaica as
'extravagantly overdone'. To her, slight fluctuations and variations in the character of flint tools need not be significant, but
may be accounted for by local factors. This is true of course,
but are not local factors of historical interest? Documentary
historians are learning to accept that many grand generalizations have to be modified because of the detailed work of local
historians, and it is surely necessary for archaeologists to do
the same. Jacquetta Hawkes also bewails the lack among
the younger generation, of people, like Childe, Wheeler,
Christopher Hawkes, Piggott and Grahame Clark, who could
synthesize and 'distil history from the welter of disparate facts'.
However, it may well be the case that, as in the field of history,
synthesis on a grand scale is no longer possible because of the
amount of archaeological material to be studied. Furthermore,
there are some people who believe that, as the standards of
excavation and analysis have risen and are now more rigorous
than they were, archaeology is starting afresh in a new fact-
finding phase, and that evidence gathered, let us say, more than
ten years ago is virtually useless; only later, when much more
information has piled up by the new standards of investigation,
will it be possible to begin extracting history. In some places
the 'let's start again' attitude is common, and one can see good
reasons for this species of puritanism. Yet there is one grave
objection: interpretation is inevitably part of the fact-finding
process, and the archaeologist is no more able than the historian
to pile up objective facts. When the argument is taken to its
logical conclusion, it becomes a prescription for isolation;
nobody should be trusted, and because standards will go on
rising nobody will trust us. In any academic discipline there
must be some trust and mutual respect, and a realization that
subjectivity will always be present in the scholarship of any
period.

Another criticism of modern archaeology, voiced by historians
and others, is right on target. They point out that the general
standard of writing is woefully poor. Reports are too often
turgid, hastily written, and full of ugly jargon. Consider this
example from a highly important recent book, which at half
its length would have been twice as effective: 'the pecularity or

singularity of archaeology then becomes apparent as residing in its role of studying fragments of solidified and preserved hominid behaviour patterns'. This habit of stringing together nouns is a most distressing aspect of archaeological English.

Historians have often remarked on the tendency for archaeologists to become animists – talking, that is, of things as if they had human thoughts and feelings. At times one has the mental picture of whole armies of pots scurrying across Europe or North America, occasionally marrying and producing suitably hybrid offspring. Leading archaeologists have warned against this danger often enough. Here for example are the words of R. J. C. Atkinson: 'one reads, commonly enough, that one type "has influenced" another; that one feature of a form "is responsible" for a similar feature of another form, or that a type "has evolved" in a given way, or "has migrated" from one place to another.'[19] Although the use of metaphor is to a degree perfectly acceptable, there is nevertheless a danger of endowing 'mere inanimate objects with a form of spurious life'. The archaeologist is of course trying to extract human history from inanimate objects, but he must be careful to recognize where the true humanity lies.

While on the subject of language, there is no doubt that archaeological terminology is often both irritating and amusing to the outsider. First there is the practice of naming human groups by reference to a key site, such as the Villanovan culture or the Mousterian industry, and more especially from some distinctive piece of physical equipment, for example, the Protruding Foot Beaker people, the Hog-backed Brick phase of the Pre-Pottery Neolithic at Jericho, or McDonald indented corrugated (smudged interior) ware. This is undoubtedly bizarre, but it must be remembered in all seriousness that the archaeologist has to describe human life in terms of objects and places. He has no other material. This is why he is in danger of animism; only through objects and sites can he get to the human beings who created them. The historian is in the much happier position of being able to describe, for example, the lives and personalities of the Marlborough family, rather than the 'Blenheim Culture'. Or, as Piggott wittily puts it, 'Edward the Confessor does not have to be concealed under the name of a Late Scratched-Ware chieftain'.[20]

Another danger that besets the archaeologist is that, once a term has been coined, it often becomes difficult or impossible to shed, even though later developments have shown it to be inappropriate. For example, the word 'cursus' was coined by William Stukeley in the 18th century to describe long avenues bounded by banks and ditches, which are now known to be characteristic of the Neolithic period and Early Bronze Age in Britain. The word reflects Stukeley's belief that the avenues were race-courses. He could even be right, but clearly one should not beg such a large question in one's terminology. Too often, we are tempted to use terms which imply function, and could therefore be wrong. It is far safer to use terms which are simply descriptive, but then one must be careful to choose characteristics which are salient and general. The term *henge-monument* describes a large class of circular earthworks with one or more entrances. The majority of these circles do not contain any standing features of stone or wood. Lintels (to which the term 'henge' applies) are only known at Stonehenge, and would be very difficult to prove elsewhere. Thus one extremely rare characteristic has been used to describe a large class of monuments, and several other and better diagnostic features have been ignored.

Another objection the historian may raise is that there is so much *bad* archaeology. Does this not effect the whole subject? This charge must be faced squarely. For example, every English county seems to have its quota of old-fashioned antiquaries, who may do a considerable amount of harm. They often amass collections of artifacts without keeping a proper record of their find-spots, they excavate badly, and they either fail to publish their results or publish them inadequately. In county and local journals it is still possible to find nonsensical reports and drawings. Local museums, societies and individuals do their best to influence these people, and sometimes succeed, but because of increased leisure and the glamour of the subject, new threats are appearing all the time. For example the availability of fairly cheap metal-detectors is now encouraging treasure-hunting as a commercial enterprise. Archaeologists are even being asked whether it is possible to stake out claims! Some antiquaries operate alone in great secrecy, while others work with groups of inexperienced people who are soon infected with bad habits.

None of these things are calculated to increase the average historian's respect for archaeology, and nobody can be happy with the present situation. Most academic subjects, including history, have their lunatic fringe, and probably always will have. While in most subjects, such people with their unscientific methods and wild theories can be dismissed with a smile by the serious student, the special tragedy about archaeology is that by the nature of excavation, evidence is lost and destroyed.

Most of the people who do damage are admittedly amateurs (or part-timers, to use a less emotive word). It is both the strength and weakness of archaeology that there is a large amateur contribution. Because most work in the field can only be carried out by teams of people doing a range of jobs, from the simplest like washing or marking pottery, to the complicated and interpretative like drawing the section of a trench or surveying an earthwork, professionals have to rely on the assistance and enthusiasm of part-time helpers. In addition, a lot of invaluable prospecting and recording is done by part-timers: every year scores of new sites and artifacts are found by people who know their own areas intimately. If it were not for such work, much information would be destroyed without record. The fact that some amateurs are tempted to do work for which they are un-trained and unqualified (in particular, excavation) should not blind us to the fact that others do work which is indispensable. After all, many professionals are tempted to do things for which they are not suited or qualified. Here as in other fields, it is not simply a question of amateur or professional status: it is a question of doing the things for which one has knowledge, experience and training, of learning one's limitations and working within them. For instance, it is a remarkable fact that the very people who do so much damage by unskilled excavation are often uncannily good field-workers who have a genius for spotting small surface traces – if only they could be persuaded to develop these talents, they would rapidly earn respect and standing.

There are of course quite serious and genuine differences between archaeology and history as disciplines. Archaeologists are much more willing to use the methods and results of other specialists – they have to be – in an effort to extract more in-formation from their evidence. This means that they will often display some familiarity with such subjects as geography, geo-logy, zoology, botany, physics and chemistry, as well as with certain crafts and branches of technology such as pottery-making, metallurgy and engineering. All these involve the study and analysis of material things, and the archaeologist cannot afford to ignore them. In addition he must learn to use special techniques for the recording and publishing of his evidence – for instance surveying, photography and draughtsmanship. To run a large modern excavation, a director must be able to handle people individually and collectively, to plan his overall strategy, to deploy his labour force economically and effectively. All these organizational and managerial skills are rather alien to the historian, at least as part of his work.[21]

Nevertheless, it would be regrettable if the historian allowed his natural dislike of the glamour that has come to surround archaeology to blind him to the real nature of the subject, and the attractions it holds for a wide range of people. Any archaeologist will admit that publicity and glamour have their dangers, but at the same time the historian should acknowledge that archaeology does have a popular appeal which most documentary research seems to lack. Even though they may not be serious students, many thousands of people regularly visit museums and monuments and clearly enjoy them. Having visited such places, a few begin to take a serious interest; they read publications, join societies, attend lectures and courses, go on training excavations, and in time may make distinct contributions of their own. Archaeology is clearly a very infectious subject, which since the Second World War has developed fast both as an academic discipline and as a popular pastime. All this is in great contrast to the world of documentary historians, which is relatively quiet, professional and not a little superior.

What is it about archaeology that grips specialist and non-specialist alike? Physical evidence has an appeal which is immediate, direct and uncomplicated (I say *appeal* advisedly; this is a very different thing from its meaning and historical significance). We can say, 'This is a piece of pottery which was fashioned by another human being thousands of years ago – here is the print of his thumb and the mark of his fingers. This formed part of the everyday equipment of unknown people, who ate and drank from it. I am holding an actual piece of the past in my hand. Whatever detailed construction or interpretation the experts put upon it, here is something I can believe in because it is visible and tangible.' Whereas historical evidence can strictly speaking only be appreciated internally by the intellect and imagination, an artifact or monument involves the senses as well – it can be seen, touched, measured and analyzed. It is a direct, objective and physical legacy from the past, which forms part of the present environment and which therefore makes the past curiously alive. In a sense, it abolishes time: we are completely trapped in a succession of fleeting moments which we call the present, but in the study of archaeology we contemplate objects which break through the barrier and re-present time past. Sometimes through physical evidence we are able to make contact with short-lived events, with moments of history – here the stimulus and power is even greater. For example, the bullet-hole in the wall, where William of Orange was murdered by Balthasar Gérard on July 10th 1584, is a strangely moving sight, and its impressiveness is not reduced by the fact that we only know its significance by using written sources.

It is perhaps worth noting here that, not only is archaeological evidence mainly concerned with groups, but that archaeo-logical research is much more of a group activity than its historical equivalent. The average excavation or piece of fieldwork can involve large numbers of people working in close contact. (Of course this in its turn raises problems of how to maintain consistently high standards and how to allot responsibility.) There is little doubt that the sociability of archaeological work is one reason for its popularity, especially among young persons. By contrast, although we find an increasing number of people co-operating on various aspects of history – local, demographic and parliamentary, for example – by far the greater part of documentary research is still carried out by individuals working alone.[22]

CRITICISM DIRECTED AT HISTORY

It should not be thought that because history is the senior pro-fession, historians have a monopoly of criticisms of the other side. Archaeologists equally can make trenchant comments on the way history is practised. Many of the criticisms are merely the extension of personal preferences and prejudices, but again there is usually a grain of truth in all of them. Documentary history is often regarded by archaeologists as a dull, dry pur-suit, lacking excitement and carried out by rather desiccated people, who immure themselves in libraries and dusty reposi-tories. This view of the historian as a troglodyte with silicosis of the lungs is quite widespread. A medieval archaeologist of the writer's acquaintance once confided that he had secured the services of a 'tame' historian who quarried documentary references for him. All he had to do was to wait for the references, and then sally out into the field to find the sites. What was so extraordinary about this attitude was the assumption that the one job was essentially more interesting than the other, and that presumably, had the historian not been at his beck and call, this archaeologist would never have bothered to do the documentary work himself.

All the same, it is true that historians make far more of a 'mystery' of their profession than archaeologist do. They are more tempted to find their subjects, work away at them myopically for years, publish papers and books, exchange information with people working on the same or related topics, and generally to live in an 'ivory tower'; there is far less contact with the man-in-the-street. An archaeologist cannot be withdrawn to the same extent – he inevitably comes into contact with landowners, farmers, farm-workers, contractors, navvies, amateur helpers, newspaper reporters and many others. He has to converse with these people, and explain his activities to them, which can be a rather humbling experience! It is entirely salutary for all academic work to be occasionally held up to public view and even ridicule, because it makes one think of the social value and relevance of what one is doing. Admittedly the pursuit of knowledge justifies itself, but at the same time history is of enormous contemporary and social relevance as a body of knowledge, and above all as a technique for distilling truth. One only has to look at the average 'current affairs' programme on television to realize how soon the truth is clouded, and how much the analytical and rational qualities derived from historical experience are needed. Nevertheless historians are for the most part strangely reluctant to explain their interests to the outside world.

The historian, as part of his mystery, is prone to exaggerate the technical difficulties of his work. For example it is often said or implied that medieval palaeography is a job for the trained expert alone. Practical classes in Local History sponsored by Extra-Mural Departments and the W.E.A. show that it is possible for intelligent adults to learn to read medieval documents by part-time work over two years or so. This is not to say that they could master all the intricacies of historical interpretation or diplomatic, but at least they are able to read, translate and discuss these sources as part of an historical project. There is a very good case for persuading all academic historians to teach at least one extra-mural group each winter – the experience could do nothing but good all round.

Although their interests are often more remote chronologically, it is a strange paradox that archaeologists are involved to a much greater extent in contemporary issues than are documentary historians. This is presumably because their interest in the physical environment inevitably brings them into contact with the everyday world of commerce, industry, government and planning. They are necessarily concerned about the character of towns, villages, buildings, monuments and other sites, and feel compelled to defend their historical and other qualities when threatened. For example, in 1965 the Council for British Archaeology which exists to co-ordinate archaeology nationally, produced an important list of historic towns worthy of special protection, with some analysis of their visual and historical qualities;[23] while in 1971 a special trust called *Rescue* was set up by leading archaeologists to bring before the public and government the unprecedented destruction of our archaeological heritage in Britain.

The attitude of some archaeologists to documentary history may be coloured by the nature of the local and regional history they come into contact with. Many a keen archaeologist, one suspects, has consulted local antiquarian works and parish histories, and has been repelled by their dullness and lack of physical awareness. Until not so long ago, most parish histories were written, as W. G. Hoskins has said, 'by gentlemen for gentlemen'.[24] They therefore contain the things that were of interest to the land-owning class, 'its pedigrees, heraldry, possessions and appendages like the parson and the church; though occasionally a more imaginative writer would devote a page or two to the conditions of the labouring class.' As we have already seen, this is partly owing to the official and legal nature of many written records, but it is also the result of the limited objectives of so much historical work.

It is often said by historians that archaeology is an ancillary aid to the study of history. Here for example are the words of H. P. R. Finberg: 'Archaeology has revealed itself more plainly as the ancillary discipline it really is: in other words as a combination of highly specialized techniques, the true and ultimate function of which is to illuminate the subject-matter of History.'[25] Archaeology is here seen primarily as a method, whereby the physical world is used in the service of history (in the broad sense). To most people this seems a fair description, but why is not documentary history seen in the same light? Is it not also a technique for assessing a distinctive form of evidence, namely written and spoken statements? If there is anything which binds historians together, it is not their period or particular study, but their craft or 'combination of highly specialized techniques'. Yet historians frequently overlook this, and assume that the history which they represent is in some way the all-embracing record of the past. Here are the words of a respected British historian: 'The historian is concerned with the totality of evidence, and with the totality of the past: the archaeologist, if he sticks narrowly to his trade, is concerned only with bits and pieces of the one and a small part only of the other. It follows that whereas the historian ought to be an archaeologist also, the archaeologist *tout court* can never be an historian.'[26] This is astonishing arrogance, which completely confuses history in the narrow sense (a technique used by the ordinary historian for extracting meaning from verbal evidence) with history in the broad sense (the record of the past from all sources).

It is natural of course that people trained in different disciplines should find each other's territory strange and unfamiliar; it only becomes a serious matter when this alienation takes the form of an inability to appreciate the claims of the other subject. Witness the totally inaccurate and derogatory definition recently given by a young archaeologist (my italics), 'History, as we know it, draws on *literary* sources and mainly *weaves its tales* around prominent individuals and *their wars*'.[27] A recent controversy in a British journal between an historian and an archaeologist gives another excellent illustration of the lack of sympathy and understanding between the two disciplines.[28] It ran as follows: 'Historians', said the archaeologist, 'are aloof and have a "master-race" mentality.' 'Archaeologists', said the historian, 'suffer from "folie de grandeur" and must remember who they are. All those bits of pot . . .'

Again and again a perfunctory reference to evidence of the other sort reveals that the writer simply does not appreciate how the other discipline works. Archaeologists often naively assume that any statement can be taken at its face value, and where a statement conflicts with physical evidence it is coolly rejected as false. On the other hand historians often refer to physical objects with equally touching innocence, and assume for example that an object found near a site automatically dates it.[29]

INTERACTION AND CO-ORDINATION

One of the most important contacts between the two subjects is that archaeological excavation and field-work have greatly increased the range of strictly historical evidence, and have thereby focussed attention on the true character of both disciplines. Archaeologists have literally dug up thousands of new documents. For example in the study of ancient civilizations such as the Sumerian, Babylonian, Egyptian, Hittite and Mycenaean, archaeologists have recovered not only houses, pottery, tombs and weapons but documents written or inscribed on a variety of materials. Generally these are on clay tablets or stone, but occasionally softer materials have survived – as in the case of the Dead Sea Scrolls. In approximately two centuries, archaeology has in fact lengthened documentary history by about two millennia.

By co-ordination we mean the attempt to use both historical and archaeological evidence in the elucidation of some historical subject or problem: that is, to study each kind of evidence by the specific methods of historians and archaeologists, and then to weld the results into a single historical account. Now why do we bother to attempt this? After all, the professions are trained separately, and there is plenty of work to be done separately. As G.R. Elton has said, 'few men, thoroughly soaked in the waters of one historical pond, feel inclined to swim in another.'[30] We bother, surely, because the evidence which exists is fragmentary and uneven. We are studying the past by means of present traces; when compared to the actual events of the past, these traces are few enough, and we shall never be able to recover more than part of the truth. As historians we have a moral duty to find out as much of the truth as possible, and should therefore be prepared to use whatever evidence survives. If it is of different kinds, then we must use it in all its variety, and co-ordinate it.

It will perhaps be objected by some people that co-ordination is dangerous because nobody can be master of more than one discipline: if the attempt is made, it will only result in superficial work, which in these days of increasing specialization is unacceptable. On the contrary, the necessity for co-ordination is a *result* of increasing specialization. As scholars are, for a variety of reasons, driven to specialize in ever smaller areas of study, so they are induced to take into account all evidence bearing on their problems, from whatever source it may come.

It is here worth recapitulating on the nature of a document, because in a sense a single document is the best example we can find of the co-ordination of historical and archaeological evidence. The object is the 'vehicle' of the message in both space and time: the message simply could not exist, were it not for the object which bears the symbols, and the symbols which are the message in frozen or fossilized form. Put the other way round, there is no historical statement without physical symbols to express it, and there are no symbols without a physical object to carry them. All three elements – objects, symbols and message – must be regarded as indissoluble, for a document cannot lack any one of them. Each element throws light on the others, and all are considered in the full interpretation of a document. If for example the handwriting of a medieval charter seems wrong for the stated date, then one suspects a forgery and begins to see the message and the object in a different light.

An object must be contemporary with or earlier than the symbols it carries. Although in the majority of cases objects are contemporary with their symbols, this must not be assumed; it is quite common for legends to be added to objects of earlier date. For example, interpolations in later hands are often found in manorial surveys, showing how property has descended since the original survey was taken. In the architectural field, dates, initials and inscriptions are often added to buildings long after they were originally built. This is of course quite elementary stratification applied to a wider field than usual. To turn to the statements, they too in most historical documents are contemporary with the relevant symbols, but this is not invariably so. Classical and medieval texts which have been copied and re-copied many times immediately spring to mind. While symbols can only be contemporary or later than the object, statements can be earlier than both. (See pp. 110-11)

But co-ordination in the usual sense is an attempt to relate written statements to physical evidence *other than their own 'vehicles'*. A good example is the indentification by Brian Hope-Taylor of the extensive 7th-century site at Yeavering, Northumberland, with the royal palace of King Edwin mentioned by Bede as *Ad Gefrin*. Basically the argument runs as follows: Ad Gefrin is probably the root of the modern place-name Yeavering, and at Yeavering extensive archaeological remains have been found which seem best interpreted as a royal palace. An historically named place is, in other words, convincingly identified with a physical site. Historical and linguistic evidence seem to focus on a particular place; all the evidence appears to agree territorially and chronologically. This kind of co-ordination – the identification of a name with a place – is common and seems relatively straightforward. For example, it has been extensively used by economic historians in the study of lost villages, and by military historians in the study of battle-fields. Perhaps the most famous example of all time was Heinrich Schliemann's identification in 1871 of Homer's Troy. He achieved a lifelong ambition by satisfying himself and the world of scholarship that the mound of Hissarlik overlooking the Dardanelles is the famous city mentioned in the *Iliad*. His subsequent excavations supplemented the Homeric story invaluably, by showing that Priam's city was only one of nine sandwiched on top of each other.

When they are fully analyzed, such apparently simple examples of co-ordination turn out to be far more complicated. What we are really doing is to show that the archaeological and historical evidence is concordant, or rather not discordant, and could therefore apply to the same places or events. We are not positively identifying one with the other, or exactly equating them; we are merely saying that, all things considered, this archaeological site of a certain character would theoretically fit the details given in the historical source. As no other likely candidates are known in the relevant area, it is probable or reasonably certain that the site and the historical place are one and the same. In later periods, such as the medieval and modern periods of European history, there are occasions when the probability of identification becomes a near-certainty, but it never becomes fully proven, because we are dealing with two basically different kinds of experience. An archaeological site and a series of statements are so unlike that they cannot simply be added to each other. When therefore we claim to have identified Yeavering as *Ad Gefrin,* we are empirically juxtaposing two different concepts in the reasoned belief that they are related, that they are different aspects of the same subject, and in the hope therefore that they will begin to react on each other to form a superior kind of evidence. In other words each kind of evidence is interpreted with constant reference to the other, because as each provides information which may be lacking or only vaguely given in the other, they expose each other's implications and deficiencies. A co-ordinated approach must therefore produce a more complex interpretation, which is surely nearer the goal of historical truth.[31]

In order to associate the two kinds of evidence in a convincing way, it is necessary for the historical statements to make some mention of the physical world (however large or small the portion concerned), and also some reference to a named locality. Let us consider an example where a surviving building is related to independent documents. In a chronicle probably written in the later 14th century by a monk of Ely, and published in 1691 by Henry Wharton in his *Anglia Sacra*, there are several descriptions of the building and rebuilding of parts of Ely cathedral in the Middle Ages.[32] We read for instance that in the first half of the 13th century Bishop Hugh de Northwold built the presbytery from the foundations; the work was begun in 1234 and completed in 1252. In 1322 the central tower fell 'cum tanto strepitu et fragore'. In the following 20 years the sacrist Alan de Walsingham designed and built the central tower in the form of an octagon with a stone base and timber super-structure, at a total cost of £2,400 6s. 11d. A contemporary of Alan, Brother John of Wysbeche, was largely responsible for the building over nearly 30 years of a new chapel of St Mary on the north side of the cathedral.

Any sensible person would agree that the three buildings referred to are in all probability the existing presbytery, octagon and Lady Chapel of the cathedral. As far as they go, the historical descriptions fit those parts of the cathedral *as they now appear*. When one goes into greater detail, the identification seems even more certain. The presbytery is built in Early English style, with such features as shafts of Purbeck marble, shaft-rings, lancet windows, stiff-leaf decoration, sunk trefoil panels and dog-tooth ornament – all of which would stylistically fit a date of 1220-52. Similarly the breath-taking octagon and lantern have all the hall-marks of an early-14th-century structure with features of the Decorated style such as foliated capitals and curvilinear tracery. Lastly, the battered but still magnificent Lady Chapel is surely one of the most widely-quoted examples in Britain of the Decorated style: its carving, particularly internally, is lavish, with such features as richly crocketed gablets, 'nodding' ogee arches, flowing tracery and lierne vaults.

This identification is worth considering more deeply. The statements made in the document may be inaccurate in certain small details, but the general gist is surely acceptable: that for example the central tower did fall, and was replaced by a stone octagon and wooden lantern during the period 1320-40. We suppose that the octagon now to be seen at Ely is the one described by the chronicler, because its style fits the date. But how do we know that the Decorated style is characteristic of the early 14th century? Archaeological typology merely suggests that the Decorated style is a development of the Early English, and is technically more adventurous, but it will give no more than re-lative dating and can never pin the style to the 14th century. This can only be done by the earlier association of physical and documentary evidence. In many cases the argument is dangerously circular: it rests on other similar assumptions and putative identifications, where documentary statements have been interpreted in terms of surviving buildings, and *vice versa*. If there are enough examples where early-14th-century buildings as recorded in documents *seem* to be represented now by the Decorated style, then the identification appears more convincing – empirically and circumstantially it seems to work.

It is theoretically quite possible for later builders to have 'forged' an early architectural style, or for restorers to have rebuilt on the original lines, so there is no final guarantee that the octagon built by Alan de Walsingham is the one that survives today. Apparent age is also no final proof: it too can only be judged on the basis of earlier associations of physical and documentary evidence, and on such variables as the type of stone used, the way the structure was maintained, and weather conditions over the centuries. These reservations are philosophi-cally important and need to be recognized by those who work in this field, even though in practice no worth-while scholar would deny that the description preserved in the *Anglia Sacra* refers almost certainly to the present Octagon.

As it happens, there are other more detailed documents which describe the rebuilding of the central tower at Ely. From the period 1322-41, seven of the annual accounts of Alan de Wal-singham as Sacrist survive.[33] They itemize the usual expenditure and income of an important department of the convent, such as rents, food and drink, pittances and stipends, but towards the end of each roll is a section entitled *Custus Novi Operis*, that is, the cost of the 'new work' – particularly on the central tower which was Alan's main responsibility. Under this heading, there are mentioned the buying and carriage of great quantities of stone, timber, lead, glass and nails, and the employment of numerous craftsmen such as masons, carpenters, plumbers and glaziers. Fascinating details emerge: for example, some of the craftsmen consulted were national figures, such as the master carpenter William of Hurle who was also employed by Edward III; much of the timber was bought at Chicksand in Bedfordshire, brought overland to Barnwell near Cambridge, and then shipped to Ely. All such information means that, as we look at this astonishing and ingenious building, we understand it much better in terms of human organization.

But as with co-ordination at any level, difficulties, limitations and apparent contradictions soon emerge, and it is not possible to fully integrate all the evidence, or to answer all questions. For example, it is not always easy to see how far the building had got each year. In the Sacrist Roll from Michaelmas 1334 to Michaelmas 1335 we read that 'eight carpenters were boarded with the servants of the Lord [Sacrist] for nine weeks, for the raising of the great posts in the new choir' (*pro exaltatione magnarum postium in novo choro*). Most interpreters would probably take this as a reference to the eight large, vertical posts which form the framework of the lantern (and which technically must have been difficult to get into place, high above the crossing), but the editor of the printed version of the rolls was strongly of the opinion that the lantern had been set up several years earlier.

There has also been considerable debate among historians over the precise role which Alan de Walsingham played. It seems from the Sacrist Rolls that at the very least he was in charge of the accountancy and logistics, but one wonders to what extent he supervised the actual work, or relied on master craftsmen and consultants like William Hurle and John Attegrene. Even more interesting, how far was Alan actually responsible for the design of this unique object? The writer of the *Historia* says that, having shaken off his initial dismay and cleared the rubble, Alan 'measured out in eight divisions, with the art of an architect, the place where he thought to build the new tower'. Early writers tended to accept this statement at its face-value, but G. G. Coulton thought it more probable that Alan's 'strictly architectural work was limited to general suggestions'.[34] We shall never know the precise answer, but the fact that in his youth Alan was known as a skilled goldsmith, and that as Sacrist he was also responsible for several other building projects, suggests that he was a man of artistic sensibilities who had a deep personal interest in building. It therefore seems quite likely, as both Salzman and Pevsner have indicated more recently, that the basic design was indeed Alan's, though he may have employed a consultant to carry out the work and be responsible for the details. At least, there seems little reason to doubt that, as the chronicler suggests, Alan's personality was the main driving-force which brought the scheme to a triumphant conclusion after 20 years.[35]

The value of the association or co-ordination of the two kinds of evidence is patently obvious. The historical details, which are basically rather prosaic lists of materials and costs, would have little interest if the octagon itself did not survive: the lists become specially meaningful when they are identified with an actual place and surviving structure. Conversely, we are able to see the building not just as an object but as the result of certain recorded events, associated with absolute dates and named individuals. The octagon itself is splendid, but Alan de Walsingham's octagon, his *novum opus,* is a human triumph.

PICTORIAL EVIDENCE

Sometimes co-ordination is made easier by the existence of special documents, which deal partly with verbal statements but mainly with pictorial representations of the physical world. Examples of this category are manuscript and printed maps, plans and elevations of buildings, water-colours, prints, tapestries, and of course photographs and films. These like any other documents are a blend of strictly historical and archaeological evidence, but the proportions are rather different. Because they are basically two-dimensional 'pictures' of objects, these sources have greater archaeological content and significance than purely written ones.

The student has to study lines, shapes, spaces and colours, and interpret them as people, buildings, roads, fields, animals and so on. Although some of these representations are, like maps, purely static and descriptive, others depict specific *events* from the past: that is to say, moments of time and physical movement are somehow captured or reconstructed. Witness for example the work of modern news-photographers in such fields as war and sport, or, to go back nearly a thousand years, the vivid representation of King Harold's death on the Bayeux Tapestry.

On the other hand the majority of these pictorial sources have at least some writing on them. Whether or not such labelling is in the form of complete sentences, it constitutes historical evidence which is invaluable for the identification of the people or areas concerned; without it the representations would be disembodied and have no connection with the real world. The small enclosed field or open strip shown on a map is not simply another example of a general kind; at a certain date it was in the tenancy of a named person, it measured a specified acreage and had a known land-use. Better still, it may be possible to 'identify' this feature in the landscape of today. Having assessed the relative accuracy of the map, and the conventions employed by the surveyor, one may decide that a certain hedged field is in all probability the very one depicted on the map; its size, shape and surroundings are today very close to the pattern delineated in the past. As in the case of Ely cathedral, we have no final proof – the apparent similarity may be accidental, because lines on a map are essentially different from hedges on the ground, and the inaccuracy of early cartographers often makes precise correlations difficult. Nevertheless there will be details on any old map which historians will consider to all intents and purposes 'identifiable' today.[36]

It merits mention that all the pictorial sources have one serious limitation: whereas it is at least possible for a written document to describe a process going on over a period of years (for example, enclosure) an individual map or print is necessarily an impression of one moment of time. Although it probably depicts features which are in process of change, it does not specify this change or its direction. Only when, for example, he has several maps covering the same area at different dates, is the historian able to measure movement in time.

This digression on 'pictorial' sources is an important reminder that the constituent elements within documents do not have constant proportions: the amount of verbal and non-verbal information varies, and so does the time which has to be spent on each. If one properly enlarges the definition of documents to include such things as stone inscriptions and inscribed brasses, the balance between the constituent elements varies even more. With most written documents, the statements are likely to be much more important than the 'vehicle' – simply because the physical character of the document, and the style of writing, will conform to a general type and appear ordinary and genuine. Clearly this is an important pre-condition, but once one is satisfied, it is the message which claims more attention. However, in the case of a forgery it may be the physical evidence which is crucial, and considerable time will have to be devoted to it – for example one may be able to show that key words have been erased or altered. With an inscribed stone, the archaeological evidence may take up at least as much time as the historical. Similarly an inscribed brass may be full of archaeological significance: the techniques of manufacture and engraving, details of clothing and armour, and the stylistic character of canopy and frame. The inscription may give no more than a name and date – highly important things, but not difficult or time-consuming to interpret.

CONFLICT OF EVIDENCE

In practice it is quite common for historical evidence to be in apparent conflict with archaeological evidence. For example several people have pointed out that the distribution of pagan Anglo-Saxon burials in southeastern England during the 5th to 7th centuries AD does not agree in detail with that of early Anglo-Saxon place-names which philologists have regarded as contemporary. In the counties of Essex and Sussex there are some areas with a concentration of cemeteries and few early place-names, and other areas with plenty of place-names and few cemeteries. Such apparent contradictions are misleading because they are caused not by discordant evidence as such, but by faulty interpretation on one side or both. In fact the view has already been expressed that '-ingas' names are not as early as has been believed, and it may thus be possible to make the two kinds of evidence concordant by assuming that the place-names represent a slightly later phase of colonization.[37] In addition there is always the chance that the accidents of survival and discovery may have unbalanced one or both kinds of evidence. It may well be, for example, that archaeological distributions are fragmentary and misleading, being partly at any rate the result of uneven coverage by field-workers, and in the field of history also one is often unsure just how representative or exceptional one's information may be.

Of course outright mistakes have been made in co-ordination. For example Wainwright has rightly castigated the tendency to use terms which uncritically associate different concepts.

We speak of 'Celtic fields' and 'Celtic brooches', implying that these things were used by Celtic peoples in Iron Age and Roman times. Perhaps they were, but there is no means of proving a connection between physical objects and linguistic or racial concepts. An archaeologist 'can stare at brooches as long as he likes but they will never speak Celtic to him, and will never tell him what language their wearers spoke'.[38] Co-ordination is possible, but it must be based on secure knowledge, a complete understanding of the nature of each kind of evidence, and an awareness that complete and final proof is unattainable.

Part II: Examples of Co-ordination

5 Traditional Achievements

It was not in fact until the 19th century that documentary history and archaeology began to grow apart as specializations: while historians at this time became much more conscious of original documents and the means of interpreting them, archaeologists developed and refined their techniques in the study of societies for which no or few documents survive. As a result of this determined search for higher and more scientific standards, the two groups understandably became two separate professions, each with its own distinctive mystique. But before then, and from at least Renaissance times onwards, scholars in reconstructing the past had made frequent use of physical evidence – for example buildings, funerary monuments and works of art – and had tried to relate them to historical statements. Some, like the 17th-century Benedictine monk and brilliant diplomatic historian Jean Mabillon, were obviously aware of the crucial difference between the two kinds of evidence, but this did not lead them to exclusive specialization in one or the other. In their various fields of interest, they gratefully took whatever evidence offered itself. It is the purpose of this chapter to discuss a few examples of co-ordination from these traditional and well-established fields of study.

CLASSICAL HISTORY

Historical and archaeological evidence have perhaps been used together longest in the study of the Graeco-Roman world.[1] Allowing for changing fashions and the loss of some texts, classical literature has been studied and copied, intermittently at least, ever since it was written. By contrast, the systematic study of classical monuments and artifacts is in general a much later development, and it was not until the Renaissance that a serious interest arose in classical inscriptions, sculpture and

architecture. The pioneers were people such as Ciriaco de
Pizzicolli of Ancona (1391-c.1450) who collected and published
three volumes of inscriptions, and his contemporary Flavio
Biondo of Forli (1388-1463) who wrote on the topography and
monuments of Rome and Italy.

Classical archaeology, as it developed from Renaissance times
onwards, had a marked emphasis on works of art and architecture – in the study of such a rich cultural tradition, it was
surely inevitable that early archaeological studies should be in
the form of art-history. The work of the great Johann Winckelmann (1717-68) is a good example of this emphasis. He made a
study of the sculpture and architecture of the classical world, and
published his results in two famous books, *History of Ancient
Art* (1764) and *Unpublished Relics of Antiquity* (1767-8). However, the excavations at Pompeii and Herculaneum, which
Winckelmann visited, introduced a new element which has since
developed enormously: now, so far as they can be separated,
the excavational side of classical archaeology is as important as
art-history. A further development occurred in the late 17th
and 18th centuries, when scholars such as Ezechiel Spanheim
and Joseph Eckhal founded the scientific study of coins. These
are highly important, firstly because they are physical objects
frequently found in excavations, and secondly because they often
bear writing: they therefore are an invaluable key for associating
archaeological and historical evidence. And so the subject
gradually expanded to cover the entire material culture of the
period – from humble everyday objects to works of art – and
at the same time the amount of evidence has been greatly increased as a result of deliberate excavation.

The excavational side of classical archaeology is now so
well-developed a specialization that some people are already
talking of a gulf between it and the study of traditional classical
archaeology in the shape of art-history. Whether or not this
is true, it is undeniable that classical archaeology of both kinds
has derived considerable benefit and stimulus from the written
record. In the study of a highly literate civilization, it is inevitable
that archaeology and history should interact at several different
levels.

First, classical literature brings home to us very vividly an
important point about the nature of any document, namely,
that there may be a difference in date between the document
as an object and the message written on it. The symbols can

only be contemporary with, or later than the object which carries it, but the message *qua* message could be considerably earlier in origin than the document itself. The oldest book known to us in Greek is the *Persae* of Timotheus, which was found as a papyrus in an Egyptian tomb. The poet lived in the late 5th and early 4th centuries BC, and the papyrus is 4th-century. There is no other manuscript surviving from classical times which is so close as this to the lifetime of the author.[2] In most instances one is dealing with copies, and copies of copies, which date from long after the original text was compiled. The message may therefore be many centuries older than the writing representing it, and the object carrying it.

For example, there are 24 manuscripts known of Plato's *Republic*. Of these the earliest dates to the 9th century AD and the latest to the 16th century.[3] Even the earliest is therefore some 1,300 years later than the original composition. For Tacitus' *Germania* there are 29 manuscripts, all of the 15th or early 16th century, and two early printed versions of the 15th century; all these descend from copies of a 9th/10th-century manuscript, which is known from historical evidence to have once existed.[4] There are five fragments of ancient copies of Aristophanes' play *The Clouds,* dated to the 3rd to 7th centuries AD. In addition 136 manuscripts are believed to have been written before the end of the 16th century. A modern edition has recently collated 41 of these manuscripts fully and eight selectively, plus a further 18 in print. All 67 are housed all over Europe from Cambridge to the Vatican.[5]

In the course of repeated copying and recopying over centuries, the message is inevitably corrupted. Simple copying mistakes were made, and this was easily done where there was no division between words; some copyists made their own selections and abstracts; others made interpolations, such as adding punctuation which could effect the sense of the text. The modern editor of a classical work has to study carefully the physical form and statements of all the extant versions, in order to reconstruct as closely as possible the original text. As part of this work, he should be able to postulate a *stemma* or line of descent, suggesting how later versions are derived or 'transmitted' from earlier versions.[6] Such a stemma, proposed by F. W. Hall (1913) for Caesar's *Gallic War,* is reproduced overleaf.

Many important classical texts were rediscovered during the Renaissance after centuries of neglect. Men of letters such as

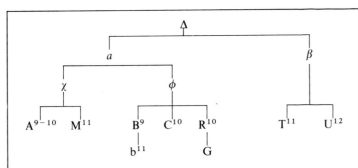

1 The Greek letters denote manuscripts no longer in existence, but judged to have existed in order to explain relationships

2 The Roman capitals denote extant manuscripts (*see key below*)

3 The numbers denote the century in which extant manuscripts were written

4 Δ denotes the ultimate archetype or common parent

Key to some of the manuscripts

A at Amsterdam, 9th-10th century
B at Paris, 9th century
M at Paris, 11th century
R in Vatican, 10th century
T at Paris, 11th century
U in Vatican, 12th century

Petrarch, Boccaccio and Pozzio searched archives and libraries, particularly at monastic houses, and having found forgotten texts, copied them and made them known to the world of scholarship. The records show that Poggio Bracciolini, a papal secretary by profession, visited monasteries in Switzerland, France and Germany, where he discovered *inter alia* texts of Cicero and Quintilian which were then unknown or only partly known.

Archaeological field-survey and excavation have extended the work begun by Renaissance scholars. Since the 18th century, and particularly since Victorian times, numerous documents have been discovered – mainly in the form of inscriptions and papyri. For the 3rd century BC, for example, about 20,000 pieces of papyri have been discovered and published, of which about 2,000 have some literary quality. They include works previously unknown, such as Aristotle's *Constitution of Athens,* the *Odes* of Bacchylides and fragments of Menander's poetry.[7]

Secondly, there are many good examples in Classical History of the way in which historical statements can be co-ordinated with objects other than their own 'vehicles'. The bodies of men, women and children at Pompeii, reconstructed by taking plaster casts of cavities in the hardened ash, become all the more poignant reminders of human suffering when one reads the younger Pliny's letters describing his experiences of human panic at Misenum, about 20 miles away on the other side of the Bay of Naples:

You could hear the shrieks of women, the wailing of infants, and the shouting of men; some were calling their parents, others their children and their wives, trying to recognize them by voice . . . the ashes began to fall again, this time in heavy showers. We rose from time to time and shook them off, otherwise we should have been buried or crushed beneath their weight . . . The buildings around us were already tottering, and the open space we were in was too small for us not to be in real and imminent danger if the house collapsed . . . We were followed by a panic-stricken mob of people wanting to act on someone else's decision in preference to their own.[8]

In addition the precise absolute date afforded by the historical source immediately gives the archaeologist a reliable peg on which to hang many kinds of artifact: we know from converting Pliny's date that the fatal eruption of Vesuvius took place on 24 August, AD 79.

Because of their regular experience of the interaction of historical and archaeological evidence, classicists have provided excellent examples of how the historical essence of archaeological findings should be extracted and presented. In the best of this work, there is a fundamental determination to talk in terms of man and human life, and to think imaginatively. These are qualities all too rarely seen in the field of prehistory. Consider this description by the late Sir Ian Richmond of a Roman attack on the native hill-fort of Hod Hill (Dorset), based largely on excavational evidence.[9] He has produced a brilliant and convincing narrative in terms of human experience and specific events. He may be wrong in certain details, but surely any student of archaeology must admire the way in which he has made mute objects speak of the past.

Small wonder, then, if hearts quailed when the Roman legionaries, with all the prestige of a successful *Blitzkrieg* behind them, approached the hill and began to reconnoitre the position. Such were the circumstances in which fate decreed that a chieftain's hut, recognizable from afar by its enclosure, if not by other distinctive features, should be situated not only within range of a *ballista* firing across the native rampart, but opposite the south-east shoulder of the hill, where the slope provided a stance for the machine and its firing-platform or for a siege-tower carrying it. To bring about a surrender, whether in the light of intelligence received or in the hope that intimidation would succeed, an obvious preliminary course of action would be to bombard the chieftain's dwelling. The shooting was good, demonstrating then and now the deadly and devastating precision with which the *ballista* can be handled. The lack of evidence for an assault on the hill-fort, or for subsequent devastation within it, would strongly suggest that capitulation was there and then induced, by showing dramatically what concentrated fire could do.

Finally, it is important to reiterate that much of the historical evidence used by the classical historian is not of the 'normal' kind (written on paper, parchment, papyrus, etc.), but is inscribed on stone and other hard materials. Yet the latter are just as much documents as the former, because they too are physical objects which bear writing. The inscription on Titus' Arch in Rome, erected in AD 81 to commemorate the capture of Jerusalem, is as much *historical* and *documentary* as is Josephus' unforgettable written account of the campaign. (This is not, of course, to say that as historical evidence they are of equal value.) To study this inscriptional evidence, both as objects and statements, the specialization called epigraphy has arisen.

DIPLOMATIC

In an earlier chapter, the significance of the science of diplomatic was mentioned. It is designed to test the authenticity of historical documents. Ever since this specialization was developed, mainly in the 17th century by men like Jean Mabillon, considerable emphasis has always been placed on the physical attributes of documents – for example, the material used, the condition, styles of writing, and seals – as well as on the message or statements. Indeed it was Mabillon's major achievement that he was able to demonstrate the authenticity or otherwise of documents by a study of physical form and style. In his *De Re Diplomatica* (1681), which includes facsimiles, he first put the study of scripts on a scientific basis.

As the word 'diplomatic' implies, most of the documents assessed in this way have been of an official nature. They were for legal and administrative purposes, and therefore tend to follow set forms. Mabillon for example wrote his great book in defence of certain Merovingian charters, whose authenticity had been impugned by a scholar called Daniel Papebroch. Such documents are studied to ensure that their archaeological and historical character is consistent both internally and by comparison with other documents.

In the well-known series of Oxford charters published in facsimile by H. E. Salter in 1929, are several which he exposed as fraudulent.[10] A case in point is the grant of a piece of land called Denescroft by Thomas le Den to St George's Chapel; this purports to be about 1130 in date, but Salter noted that 'from the handwriting we should date it more than a century later'. Similarly the seal 'is of a style which was very common about 1220-1240'. Here the physical character of the writing and of the seal is found to be inconsistent with the alleged historical statement. Salter concluded that this and other deeds in the same hand 'seem to have been made about 1230 or 1240 to supply a good title for the land which Oseney abbey obtained from the chapel of St George'.

Perhaps one of the best popular descriptions of the diplomatic process is T. F. Tout's lecture in 1919 on the fraudulent *History of Crowland,* which because it was formerly supposed to have been written by Abbot Ingulf in about AD 1089 is known as the 'pseudo-Ingulf'. In devastating, historical language Tout illustrates abundant internal and external inconsistencies, mainly historical but sometimes archaeological in nature.[11]

To begin with, there is no manuscript of the chronicle older than the sixteenth century. The 'autograph of Ingulf' which Spelman is said to have seen, has mysteriously disappeared with all the other pre-Tudor copies. The narrative and charters alike teem with all sorts of anachronisms. The place-names are in the form of the fourteenth and not of earlier centuries. The forger did not know the difference between Anglo-Saxon and Norman Latin terms. He puts earls of Lincoln and Leicester in Anglo-Saxon times and calls Saxon nobles after the names of castles founded by Normans. He makes Thurketil the chancellor of Edward the Elder, though the first English king to have a chancellor was Edward the Confessor. He says that the triangular bridge, a fourteenth-century structure, existed in the tenth century. He puts fiefs, manors, sheriffs, archdeaconries, seals, vicars, into ages which knew them not. He sends dead men on missions to kings and princes; he makes Ingulf on his travels visit an emperor who was not yet an emperor, and a patriarch who was already in his grave. He makes Thurketil recommend as bishops people who died years before he was born. He makes aged monks, driven away by the heathen Danes, come back to restore the abbey and resume their monastic routine, and die, years afterwards, at such ages at 148, 142 and 115. He makes Ingulf study in the non-existent University of Oxford the metaphysics of Aristotle at a time when that work was unknown in Western Europe . . .

SEALS

Within the larger subject of diplomatic, the study of seals
(sigillography) provides a good example of the co-ordination
of archaeological and historical evidence, both within the scope
of a single document and outside it.

Following the definition of Hilary Jenkinson, a seal is an
'addition to a written document of an impression, generally
in some mixture of bees-wax, from a finger-ring or some larger
surface, identifiable by the device or wording engraved on it
as the property of a particular person' or institution.[12] In this
sense the Papacy had been using seals since at least the 6th,
and rulers in Europe from the 10th century AD. It was a visual
and non-verbal guarantee that the document had come from the
implied source in a period when most people were illiterate,
often including the ones for whom and to whom the documents
were written. The word 'seal' is used to describe both the
impression and the tool (die or matrix) which made it. It is the
impression of course which usually survives for study.

In practice, then, a seal is generally a flat disc of wax bearing
impressions on one or both sides. The design of these impressions
varies enormously, but in general it consists of pictorial representations and symbols, often accompanied by writing. It is
therefore a combination of verbal and non-verbal evidence,
like the epigrapher's inscription and, indeed, like any other
class of document.

Here is the description which Jenkinson makes of a very
beautiful seal, which for various historical reasons we know to
be that of Earl John de Warenne in 1347.[13] Notice that for the
most part he is speaking entirely archaeologically, but how the
briefer historical references are of enormous significance to the
full interpretation of the artifact.

An impression in dark green wax from a round, double matrix, a little
over four inches in diameter, appended by plaited laces of red and lilac
silk to Letters Patent dated 1 April, 20 Edward III by which John de
Warenne, Earl of Surrey, and Stratherne, granted to the king certain
castles, towns and manors in Surrey, Sussex and Wales. The seal is
of Royal size and character, doubtless because of the owner's Palatine
position in regard to his Earldom of Stratherne. The *Obverse* shows
the Earl in robes, seated on a throne, panelled and carved, and holding
a flower in his right hand: the background in allusion to his family
name, consists of a warren, with rabbits, a hart, etc.: *Legend
– +Sigillum: Johannis: Comitis: Warennie: et Strathernie: et Comitis:
Palacii* in Lombardic capitals. The *Reverse* shows the Earl in armour,
on horseback, galloping to the right; the horse's trapper and the Earl's

shield and ailette displaying the chequered device of Surrey; the background, similar in character to that of the obverse, shows a pool with swan and cygnets and storks: *Legend— + Sigillum: Johannis: Comitis: Warennie: et: Surr* . . . A good impression, but about a quarter of the seal (in the right, as one looks at the Obverse) has been broken away and the Earl's left fore-arm (on the Reverse, his right fore-arm with sword) is missing: together with some of the legend in each case.

The existence of the historical information means that extra significance can be read into the physical object itself. Thus, knowing the name of the owner of the seal, one can see a symbolic and punning significance to the 'warren' of rabbits, hart, swan, cygnets and storks. What were simply small, decorative details of design are now charged with a higher meaning, which it would otherwise have been impossible to recover. The phrase 'the chequered device of Surrey' conceals an equally complicated co-ordination of historical and archaeological thinking. From various other 'documents' – writings, labelled heraldic drawings, tombs, brasses – we know that the chequer pattern is heraldically associated with the Warenne family, Earls of Surrey.

In the standard works on seals, one is struck again and again by considerations which are essentially similar to those of every archaeologist. There is the usual problem of nomenclature – the imprecision of terms and lack of standardization. For example, the words, label, pendicle, tag and tongue have all been used for the cut strip of parchment on which seals are often placed. Then there are the problems of dating seals which are no longer attached to dated parchments. Here of course various typological criteria are brought into play. For instance, by using seals which were associated with written dates, it was long ago demonstrated that there was a general progression in styles of lettering, from the early use of Roman capitals, to Lombardic script, to 'black letter', and back to Roman capitals. Again, some indication of date may well be given by details of costume and armour, of architecture and of styles of heraldry. Although this kind of dating is only very approximate, it is more reliable than the purely relative dating of the prehistorian, because an ultimate connection with written dates of an absolute kind can always be found.

One very important point about the date of seals is that the impression which one usually studies is not only, quite obviously, later than the date of manufacture of the matrix (or die), but can be considerably later. This is particularly true of corporations such as boroughs, colleges, and schools, where matrices are often used without change for a long time.

Because the study of seals is basically a kind of archaeology within the world of documentary history, it suffers from historians' prejudices. Generally it is the more 'important', 'interesting', and 'beautiful' seals which have been studied, that is, those that belong to the more prominent and powerful members of society. Yet there are thousands more surviving from the 13th century onwards, which belonged to people relatively low in the social scale, and which need far more attention than they have so far received.

The purpose of seals was to give authenticity; but the fact remains that they were sometimes forged and used fraudently. There are of course different grades of forgery, not all equally culpable. At one extreme are documents, like the pseudo-Ingulf, in which everything was fabricated. In other cases genuine seals were attached to forged documents, sometimes to support long-standing claims and sometimes to replace documents genuinely lost or destroyed. C.N.L. Brooke has described two remarkable late-12th-century papal bulls, which apparently granted indulgences for the benefit of the nuns of Wix Priory (Essex).[14] The parchments on palaeographic grounds are patently false, because the handwriting does not belong to the papal chancery, and is apparently the same as in many of the early Wix charters in the Public Record Office. Yet the bulls proper (lead seals) with all their fine detail appear to be genuine issues of Pope Celestine III (1191-8).

Brooke goes on to describe how such forgeries were carried out. 'One technique . . . is to take a genuine bull, cut of the seal, and reattach it to a spurious document. This involves . . . cutting the strings and retying them in such a way as to hide the join; or else heating the top of the lead bull or seal, inserting the strings coming from the new, bogus parchment, and then closing the top of the seal again with pincers.' As far as the two Wix charters are concerned, it is just possible to detect the marks of the forger's pincers on one of the bulls, though not on the other. 'These are the work of highly qualified professionals,' remarks Brooke. Here we have a good example of an historian thinking archaeology: the Wix charters were proved to be forgeries, not by their historical content and meaning, but by a careful study of the physical form of the writing, and the way in which the seal had been fraudulently attached.

Heraldry

Heraldry can take many physical forms and may turn up in many different contexts.[15] It is basically a complicated system of designs involving lines, shapes and colour, usually in two-dimensional, but sometimes in three-dimensional form. The fundamental shape is the pointed shield, which was characteristic of the 13th century. On this are put geometrical shapes called 'ordinaries' (such as the cross, chevron and bar) and 'charges' which can be representations of any object, animate or inanimate, real or imaginary (the most common being probably birds, animals and flowers). For a full 'achievement' the shield is surmounted by a helmet, crest and mantling, and supported to left and right by human or animal figures. Occasionally the design of the shield involves writing, as for example the Black Prince's shield for peace which consisted of three ostrich feathers passing through scrolls bearing the words 'Ich Dien' (I Serve). From late medieval times onwards it was also common for a full achievement to rest on a scroll bearing a motto.

Coats of arms were applied in a variety of techniques to many kinds of artifacts and documents. They can be found carved on buildings and tombs; engraved on brasses; impressed on seals; painted on glass, plaster, wood and canvas; drawn and painted on paper and parchment. Nowadays they are commonly painted on vans, lorries and buses, and can even be formed of flowers on municipal lawns!

Heraldry sprang up in medieval Western Europe from the need to recognize armoured knights engaged in tournaments and warfare. Coats of arms generally have no actual meaning, though occasionally there is a punning or historical reference: their primary purpose was simply to be distinctive. They were hereditary symbols by which individuals and families were to be distinguished in a systematic, visual way. The verbal motto may have originated in the *cri de guerre* or watch-word.

To historians, heraldry would have remained a series of pleasing designs, but unidentifiable in terms of persons and families, had it not been that in some contexts coats of arms can be physically related to written names and dates. Three main categories of document are able to provide this invaluable association. First, there are various written sources such as Rolls of Arms and the records of heraldic Visitations: some of these give painted or 'tricked'[16] illustrations of shields, labelled with names, while others give purely verbal descriptions in a special technical language. Secondly, there are heraldic seals which are either themselves labelled, or associated with the written message of the attached document. Thirdly, there are funerary monuments such as tombs and brasses, where heraldry often features with a written message. These associations enable the heraldic expert to put a name to individual designs, and to identify unlabelled examples by cross-reference to labelled ones.

Although most arms were designed simply to be distinctive, some have an extra significance. Some devices make clear historical allusions, by using objects as charges which are related to the lives of their owners. For example the heart on the Douglas shield commemorates the unsuccessful attempt of Sir James Douglas to take the heart of Robert the Bruce to Jerusalem. In the achievement of Thomas Wolsey were a cardinal's hat and archiepiscopal cross. In other cases, there is a clear punning or 'canting' significance: for instance, a castle for Oldcastle and a spear for Shakespeare. Obviously one cannot appreciate these visual puns or allusions, until one knows from related historical evidence the people involved.

As designs, coats of arms can be related to one another in various ways. To take an example: J. H. Round has made out a convincing case for the arms of several families such as Say, Beauchamp of Bedford, Clavering, Very and Lacy being derived from the arms of their common ancestor Geoffrey de Mandeville: similarities of design coincide with genealogical connections known from historical sources.[17] There are many coats which seem to be based on others already existing, and which may therefore represent connections by kinship or tenure. By the process known as 'marshalling', two or more coats can be fused. This may involve impalement (the shield vertically divided into halves), or quartering (the shield divided into quarters), or superimposition (a small shield placed in the centre of a larger one). The reasons for marshalling can be marriage, descent, the holding of certain offices, and the union of lordships.

In the course of time, the non-verbal symbolism of heraldry became more complex. In the late Middle Ages, for example, small 'cadency' marks were added, to distinguish the cadets from the head of a family. The eldest son, during his father's lifetime, carried a label; the second son carried a crescent; the third a star. From Elizabethan times, social rank was indicated by different patterns of coronet. A duke's coronet bore eight strawberry leaves, a marquess' four strawberry leaves and four pearls, an earl's eight pearls and eight strawberry leaves, and so on. The symbolism as it evolved was of course organized and recorded by the Kings and Heralds of Arms, and after 1673 by the College of Arms. This has ensured that the symbols have been generally understood.

One of the most fascinating things about heraldry is its terminology. This was forming in the 12th and 13th centuries, and has since been made increasingly complex as new distinctions and categories have been added. Linguistically the basic words are French or anglicized versions of French. In this technical language the description of a coat of arms is called a 'blazon'. Sometimes there is some doubt as to where details should be placed, but generally the precision of the language is such that an accurate reconstruction of the coat can be made from the blazon. Here are two examples, one medieval and one modern.

The shield of Ralph Fitzranulf of Middleham is a relatively simple design, and was blazoned in Glover's Rolls of Arms (*c.* 1245) as *d'or ung chief endente d'azure;* a modern herald would render it as: *Or a chief indented azure.* In non-specialist language, this means: a pointed shield of golden colour, with an indented band at the top coloured blue.[18]

Nelson's coat of arms, confirmed in 1797, is much more complex in design and description, and comes from a period when the charges were much more varied and biographically pictorial. The blazon of the shield runs as follows: *Or a cross flory sable a bend gules surmounted by another engrailed of the field charged with three bombs fired proper on a chief (of honourable augmentation) undulated argent waves of the sea, from which a palm tree issuant between a disabled ship on the dexter, and a battery in ruins on the sinister all proper.* Most of this rather ridiculous verbiage is of course English supplementing the basic medieval terms. The blazon for the full achievement goes on to describe an extraordinary array, including a viscount's coronet, stern of a Spanish man-of-war inscribed 'San Josef', a sailor armed with a cutlass and pair of pistols, a broken flagstaff with a Spanish flag, and the motto *'Palmam qui meruit ferat'*! No wonder that Charles Boutell described these arms as a flagrant example of 'degenerate pictorial Heraldry'![19]

Of course there are illogicalities in the system. For instance, in medieval times a certain beast *rampant* was called a lion;

the same beast *guardant* was called a leopard. It is also true
that blazoning only describes a limited series of physical forms,
but nevertheless this is surely the most concise 'archaeological'
terminology yet invented.

Finally, the fascination of heraldry as a combination of
physical and written elements is underlined by the standard
books of reference. An *Armory* is an alphabetical dictionary
of families: using the personal and family name one finds the
appropriate coat of arms. By contrast, an *Ordinary* is a means
of working in the opposite direction, from the archaeology to the
history, that is, from a coat of arms to the family concerned.
Rather like a botanist's *Flora* it enables the student, by an
orderly analysis of colour and shape, to narrow down the field
and eventually identify the arms with a family or individual.

ARCHITECTURAL HISTORY

For many generations, buildings have been studied for their
historical interest. Understandably, most early historians and
antiquaries tended to concentrate on churches and 'stately
homes' – mainly because they were the largest and most imposing,
and partly because of their connection with the more powerful,
wealthy and articulate elements in society. Such buildings
as these had relatively large sums of money spent on them,
and were therefore of considerable stylistic refinement. This
meant that they could be studied typologically, and that there
was a chance of finding written documents, prints and drawings
which could provide information about their original erection
and subsequent history. Indeed, if documents relating to a
building exist, the specialist has a responsibility to use them.
So it has become recognized that 'to be fully equipped as an
architectural historian, it is necessary to master two distinct
techniques – the technique of finding, reading and interpreting
documents, and the technique of analyzing the style and structure of buildings'.[20]

In the main, the buildings with which the architectural historian
is concerned are still inhabited or used, but some can be in various
stages of dereliction and ruin. As they are physical 'monuments'
of the past, there is no difficulty in seeing them as archaeological
in nature; buildings are complex, man-made artifacts which
can be analyzed, classified and dated, using the fundamental
principles of all kinds of archaeology.

The application of typology is obvious at several points – in the external form of buildings (for example basilican and cruciform plans of churches), in the internal form (for example, open halls and halls at first-floor level), and in stylistic detail (for example, window tracery, mouldings, and the structure of roofs). The architectural historian usually has the great added advantage of being able to tie his types, directly or indirectly, to documentary evidence; because of this architectural typology has become a matter of absolute rather than relative dating. An architectural feature has a precise date when it was made, but as a type it may have been current for a long period, and specialists are always concerned to find the upper and lower chronological limits. Stratigraphy is of course normally applied to the successive layers of soil encountered in an excavation, but as it is essentially a means of distinguishing earlier from later elements by their relative positions, it can be used above-ground as well. For instance, a blocked window obviously shows a later modification to the original structure, or, to put it in utter simplicity, the window must have been there before it was blocked.

The most commonly encountered indication of different periods in a building is a 'straight-joint', that is, a line where two areas of walling of different dates are set directly against one another. For example, it is common for aisles to be added to an originally box-like church, or for new wings to be added to a large house: in these cases, there is often a straight vertical line where the addition abuts the original core. Occasionally there is some doubt as to which part of the building is new and which old, especially when both elements are similar in style and of comparable size. Generally, however, the additions are obvious because they are stylistically later, and are three-sided (in the sense that they make use of the original structure for the fourth side). Again, buildings were commonly raised in height, for example when a clerestory was added to the nave of a church: in these cases, a horizontal straight-joint can sometimes be seen on the main walls marking the junction between old and new, while at the gable-ends there may be a sloping joint. Assuming gravity had not been curiously defied, there is no doubt here as to which part is old and which new. In general, then, architectural stratigraphy is practised above-ground, but because it lacks the enveloping matrix of soil with its informative system of layers the total stratigraphic information available for a standing building is inferior to that of an excavated one.

The historical evidence relating to buildings is very diverse. In the first place, there is sometimes an inscription on the building itself. This is most commonly a date, or a series of initials, but it can occasionally be a much longer and more explicit statement, recording an event or commemorating a person. It should never be assumed that an inscription is necessarily of the same date as the building to which it is attached: very often it turns out to be a later addition recording, say, a change of ownership or a restoration. Sometimes early inscriptions were incorporated, either accidentally or deliberately, in a later building – the well-known Roman tombstones in the crypt of Hexham Priory provide an example of this. As with most kinds of 'document', the contemporaneity of the historical message and its physical vehicle cannot be assumed: the inscription can be contemporary with, or later than, or even earlier than, the part of the building to which it is attached.

For historical evidence bearing on the great majority of buildings, one must hope to find independent documents. One thinks of the importance of locally-written chronicles and fabric rolls for the history of cathedrals and abbeys (the example of Ely cathedral has already been discussed in Chapter 4), of licences-to-crenellate for castles and manor-houses, of wills and churchwardens' accounts for parish churches, and of contracts and prints for country houses. Information relevant to buildings can turn up in almost any kind of document, and there is no doubt that, as architectural historians have accustomed themselves to the use of historical evidence, the study of buildings has become more precise.

A remarkable early example of co-ordination in the field of architectural history was provided by the talented John Aubrey in the 17th century. In an unpublished work called *Chronologia Architectonica* he attempted to work out the sequence of architectural styles in medieval England, with reference to dated college buildings at Oxford. Many years later came T. Rickman's *An attempt to discriminate the styles of English architecture from the Conquest to the Reformation* (first published in 1817). The first five editions were basically an exercise in the detailed typology of medieval architecture: Rickman worked out the sequence of styles from the architectural remains themselves, and did not discuss relevant documents to any great extent.

It was J. H. Parker who, in making substantial additions to later editions of Rickman's book, included abundant references to manuscripts, published works and lapidary inscriptions, thereby interpreting the typologies of Rickman in terms of historical dates, personalities and events.[21] Parker was not alone in this work. Robert Willis, a professor of mechanics at Cambridge, did remarkable archaeological and documentary surveys of Winchester cathedral and the buildings of Cambridge University,[22] while Wyatt Papworth in his monumental *Dictionary of Architecture* (1852-92) also made extensive use of historical sources.

In their classic study of Anglo-Saxon church architecture, H. M. and J. Taylor have summarized the achievement of these 19th-century pioneers.

For the dating of post-Conquest churches the evidence is firmly established in written records, which enable large numbers of buildings to be dated with precision, since the features which survive can be identified in detail with features described in the records as having been built at specified post-Conquest dates, often even by named persons. There is, therefore, no doubt about the general accuracy of the commonly accepted scheme of assignment of the dates at which particular styles of building were current from the latter part of the 11th century onward, although allowance must always be made for variations from place to place and also for conscious copying of earlier styles at a later date.[23]

This work of co-ordination by Parker, Willis, and others laid the foundations of ecclesiology, and stimulated a vast amount of new research and publications. It is no accident that many local and national societies in Britain were founded in the 1840s and 1850s, and that one of their main preoccupations was architectural history in general and ecclesiology in particular.

Finally, it is worth stressing that may of the fittings and contents of buildings are also strictly documents, as they frequently bear some kind of legend. In churches, there are mosaics, stained glass, wall-paintings, hatchments, bells, plate, vestments, boards (giving charities, commandments, prohibited degrees of marriage, etc.) and above all, funerary monuments such as tombs, grave-slabs and brasses. All these by their mixed nature can provide opportunities for further co-ordination. For example, it is an inscribed tomb in Southwark cathedral, London, which enables a biographer to identify John Gower the medieval poet with John Gower of St Mary Overies whose will was proved in 1408. In fact, the tomb 'is the only positive identification' of the poet: the present inscription and the original (recorded by Aubrey in the 17th century) refer to John Gower as a poet, while the head of the effigy rests on three volumes inscribed with the names of Gower's principal poems.[24] In the course of history, many of these documents have been destroyed or defaced, so that our only chance of restoring the lost texts is to find transcripts or drawings made by earlier historians and antiquaries: hence the importance of works such as John Weever's *Ancient Funerall Monuments* (1631) and Richard Gough's *Sepulchral Monuments of Great Britain* (1794).

ART-HISTORY

As a final example of co-ordination, we come to a field where physical objects are endowed with an extra significance. It entails the study of works of art created by architects, sculptors and painters (as opposed to the works of men of letters and composers, which have no single or permanent physical form). We can study how they were made as objectively as in the case of any artifact, but how do we explain their purpose? In general terms a work of art was designed in order to give an emotional pleasure, to satisfy a sense of beauty, or to present a pattern of forms, materials and colours which in some way pleases us. In other words, whereas the purpose of an ordinary, utilitarian artifact is to carry out a physical function such as cutting, scraping, sawing or piercing, the purpose of a work of art is to communicate emotions. Furthermore, a work of art has a timeless significance which an ordinary artifact lacks. A stone axe was made to cut timber, and after a certain period of time was probably discarded because it was worn out, or because it had been superseded by a more efficient implement. Although fashions and tastes vary, a work of art can, and does, appeal to more than the maker and his generation.

   The distinction between the visual and abstract arts happens to be a useful parallel to the difference between archaeology and history. The messages or statements which the historian studies are, like a piece of music, purely abstract, though they too are represented by writing or notation on a physical object. The writing and the object are not the message, any more than the musical score is the symphony: they are merely the vehicle or 'key' (J. S. Ackerman's word).[25] By contrast, archaeology and art-history are primarily concerned with mute objects and their historical interpretation.

Art-history, that is the study of visual works of art, is a very wide subject which substantially overlaps the territory of the archaeologist. Indeed, by the definitions offered earlier in this book, art-history should be regarded as a branch of archaeology. It is part of the physical legacy from the past, and the fact that it represents one of the most sophisticated pursuits of the human mind, makes it the most important of all kinds of physical evidence. Within the broad field of archaeology, the art-historian concentrates on objects that were created either for entirely artistic purposes or, though functional, were artistically designed and decorated. As Talbot Rice has said, the art-historian is interested in any manifestation, however humble, of the artistic impulse – ranging from 'a work as complicated and vast as Rheims cathedral or the Sistine Chapel to that of one as small as a single pot or a minute ivory carving'.[26] Finally, it must be stressed that the repertory of art-treasures has been greatly increased by archaeological excavation: the Hermes of Praxiteles, the palace of Knossos, the contents of Tutankhamen's tomb and the famous gold discs from the sacred well of the Maya at Chichen Itza – these and thousands of other objects, large and small, have added new and unsuspected dimensions to our knowledge and enjoyment of human creativity.

The archaeologist does not simply abandon this aspect of physical evidence to the art-historian. He cannot ignore the artistic impulse in human history any more than he can ignore religion: as an historian he must weigh these in his assessment of the standards and values of life. He studies works of art by his normal methods, and also uses the findings of his specialist cousins. So in practice archaeologists and art-historians frequently study the same object, and help each other to extract meaning and significance from it.

Within art-history there are two distinct considerations which in practice overlap. First is the analysis of style and character, which is really a specialist exercise in typology; the raw materials are noted and how they were worked as shapes, tones, brush-strokes, textures, gestures and so on. Nowadays, with a growing battery of new scientific aids such as infra-red photography, this side of art-history reveals more and more of the artist's basic skills and techniques. On the basis of this knowledge, works of art are attributed to individual artists or schools, forgeries are detected, and dates assigned. Secondly, an assessment is made of the *worth* of the object. How far has the artist succeeded in conveying the idea or emotion with which he was concerned? This is of course a much more difficult task, and does not, to say the least, always lead to agreement.

Historical documents have been used by art-historians for generations. These may take the form of journals or letters written by artists, which will give information about their circumstances, states of mind, personal beliefs, and styles of life. Or they may be records relating to the works of art themselves and their treatment over the years, such as accounts, receipts, sale catalogues and household inventories. Works of criticism, which will show how much or little a particular work of art has been appreciated at different times, are also often at their disposal. Finally, there is frequently a whole range of historical sources which help to paint the background of the period, or, without mentioning it specifically, help to explain aspects of a work of art (for example, chronicles that reveal political circumstances, biblical references which help to interpret imagery, and visitation records to make sense of heraldry).

That enigmatic medieval work of art known as the Wilton Diptych provides a good illustration of the way in which historical and archaeological evidence interact in the study of a particular piece. Because of uncertainty as to its date, origin, stylistic affinities and iconography, a considerable literature has arisen over the years. Although the two wooden panels and their paintings are well known, it is worth considering in detail Francis Wormald's excellent description in the *Journal of the Warburg Institute*.[27] Notice how apparently straightforward descriptive comments do in fact contain and conceal considerable historical interpretation, and rest on independent documentary sources. As a reminder, the parts which involve historical evidence are italicized where they first occur; the rest is an objective description of physical characteristics:

The Wilton Diptych in the National Gallery in London consists of two [hinged] panels of oak painted on both sides. On the left panel of the obverse is *King Richard II* kneeling on the ground clothed in a gown ornamented with *his devices;* the crouching hart in wreaths of broom cods and flowers. He wears round his neck a collar composed of pairs of broom cods, each pair being divided from the next by a flower. On his left breast he wears *his particular badge* of the white hart. Behind him stand *St John the Baptist* and *St Edward the Confessor, King of England 1042-1066.* The latter holds a ring in his hand *referring to the legend that he gave his ring to a pilgrim who was really St John the Evangel-*

ist in disguise. On the extreme left is *another royal saint, St Edmund of East Anglia*, holding the arrow *with which he was killed by the Danes in 869*. This group of four persons is placed in a deserted landscape with a group of dark trees in the background, just visible to the right of St John the Baptist's legs. The right-hand panel of the obverse shows the *Virgin and Child* with eleven *angels* walking on a lawn covered with flowers. They are advancing on the figures in the left-hand panel. Three angels point towards the King and another holds a banner showing the red cross upon a white ground. The Christ Child appears to beckon the King with a blessing. Each of the eleven angels wears a fillet of roses, a collar of broom cods round the neck and the badge of the white hart on the left breast. Both the angels and the Virgin are dressed in blue. On the reverse of the picture on the left panel is a shield of arms showing the *mythical* arms of *Edward the Confessor* impaling the quartered arms of *France and England* surmounted by a helmet, a cap of maintenance and a crowned lion. On the right-hand panel is the white hart couched among leaves and flowers.

It would be impossible here to analyze all the subtle interactions between physical and documentary evidence in that description, but let us examine the first words italicized. All experts are agreed that the picture shows Richard II, though of course the figure is not labelled in any way. We know by many associations, physical and documentary, that the kneeling and crowned figure represents a royal personage, but why Richard II? There are in fact three main physical details in the design which, because of other physical and documentary associations, are known to be connected with Richard II.

First, there is the coat of arms on the back of the left-hand panel. From rolls of arms, chronicles and other documents we know that the shield displays the quartered arms of England and Wales impaled with those that were assigned retrospectively to Edward the Confessor. Froissart's Chronicle reveals that Richard II adopted the arms of St Edward in 1394-5 'to please the Irish', while in the *Annales Ricardi Secundi* there is a precise description of the impaled arms as shown on the diptych.

Secondly, there is the emblem of the white hart, with chain and crown, worn on the breasts of the kneeling figure and the angels. From several documents, such as *Vita Ricardi Secundi* by the monk of Evesham and the poem *Richard the Redeless*, it is known that the hart was the personal emblem or 'stigma' of Richard II, and that it was not generally worn before 1390. It also features on Richard's famous effigy in Westminister Abbey, which was made in 1395-9.

Thirdly, there are the broom cods which form a collar and

circular patterns on the robe of the kneeling figure, and are worn as collars by the angels. The broom or *planta genesta* is known from French documentary sources to have been an emblem used by French kings in the 14th century. It is recorded also that Charles VI of France on the occasion of his daughter's betrothal to Richard II in 1395-6, gave Richard and his uncles golden collars in the form of broom cods. This emblem also is prominent on Richard's effigy.

These are the main features which point to Richard II, but there are others. For example, the three saints who are presenting the King to the Virgin and Child are identifiable by their apparel and symbols, and are known to have associations with Richard. St John the Baptist was his patron saint, and he came to the throne on or about St John's day. The two royal saints, Edward the Confessor and St Edmund of East Anglia, were ancestors whom Richard greatly revered. An inventory reveals that in 1389 Richard gave to Westminster Abbey a chasuble: it was decorated with images of the Trinity, the Virgin, St John the Baptist, St Edward and St Edmund. Professor Wormald has also pointed out that near Richard's tomb in the Abbey there were chapels dedicated to the three saints represented on the diptych.

All this comparative knowledge, derived from independent documents and other objects, enables the art-historian to read meaning and significance into the painting; without it, he would only be able to guess that certain elements in the design were personal emblems, but would get no further towards the identification of a real person and a precise date. Although there are no independent documents referring to the diptych itself, there is enough comparative evidence to justify the interpretation which Wormald gave in his description. Our understanding of the diptych today rests very largely on the researches of Miss M. V. Clarke, published in 1931: it was she who first saw the full significance of the heraldry and other symbols, and argued that the diptych must have been painted after 1395. Her work is an excellent example of patient and finely-reasoned co-ordination in the field of art-history.[28]

Although the use of independent historical evidence is immensely valuable, and adds new dimensions to our appreciation of art, it does not necessarily bring total revelation – it often in fact raises completely new problems. There is, for example, considerable argument as to whether or not faces in the Wilton Diptych are actual portraits. Margaret Galway has suggested that the two royal saints may be portraits of Edward III and the Black Prince, while the Virgin may be a likeness of Richard's mother, Joan of Kent,[29] but other writers have emphatically rejected this idea. Miss Clarke's demonstration of the date after which the diptych was painted (an historically-determined *terminus post quem*) raises the new and as yet unsolved problem as to why it was painted, and for what occasion.

Much has also been written about the style of the Wilton Diptych. Since the painter is unknown, the debate has been largely about national origin. Critics have argued for various origins – Italian, Bohemian, French and English. Perhaps, as V. H. Galbraith has suggested, most experts today are in favour of it being 'an English painting by an English painter', because of the correctness of the English heraldry, the flatness of the figures and faces, and the intensely linear character of the composition, though it is still classified by the National Gallery as belonging to the French school.[30] The arguments have revolved round similarities with other works of art whose origins are known. Other scholars have introduced the idea of foreign influences. While Professor Wormald has suggested that the naturalism of the diptych attests Italian, probably Lombardic, influences, though the painting was probably done in England, Margaret Rickert has complicated the argument still further by alleging that the two panels are not part of a single composition.[31] The left-hand panel she regards as Sienese, and the right-hand as French.

Growing out of the question of style is that of the aesthetic worth of a work of art. We have already discussed how the artist's intention is to design something which gives emotional pleasure and satisfaction. Certain arrangements of forms, line and colours seem to be welded into unity and harmony, and these we accept as works of art. They are so designed that the viewer's eye is guided in a certain progression, whereby consideration of the details leads to an appreciation of the whole. Applying this to the Wilton Diptych, it has been claimed that one's eyes are led from left to right by the postures, gestures, and particularly the hands of the saints, across the shoulders of the king to the Virgin and Child, and then left and right around the circle of angels. (This analysis partly assumes of course that the two panels belong together.)

Many people have written about the appeal of the diptych. Thomas Bodkin has referred to its 'supreme loveliness' and its 'sheer beauty', while for Joan Evans it is 'without question the greatest picture of the age that is left to us'.[32] Margaret Rickert, seeking more to convey its effect on the senses, has written of a 'mystical dreaminess of mood harmonizing so perfectly with the cool colours and the softly falling draperies'. In the final analysis, one cannot of course prove that an object is beautiful. One can only say with humility that, having to some extent analyzed its construction and style, one acknowledges a mysterious and indefinable quality which synthesizes and unites all its various elements. To acknowledge a material object as a work of art is not so much to express a personal opinion, as to express a personal experience.

6 The new opportunities

By dividing the history of co-ordination into two parts, one is not suggesting that the older kind is now abandoned. On the contrary, some of the examples used in the last chapter were quite recent work, and as much is being done now as before, if not more, in classical history, numismatics, art-history and so on. But there is an important difference where more recent developments are concerned, and this derives largely from the way in which history and archaeology have grown apart as 'tunnel' specializations.

Whereas the founders of integrated studies such as art-history and classical history were prepared, where appropriate, to use all kinds of evidence (a tradition still to some extent observed by their successors today), most modern historians and archaeologists are far more rigid in their attitudes, and prefer to work exlusively on either written *or* physical evidence. Academic training has fortified these attitudes, so that a man who adopts an interdisciplinary approach largely teaches himself, and does so more in spite of, than because of, his training. This means that, although there has been a genuine revival of interest in co-ordination and interdisciplinary co-operation in the past 25 years, involving the creation of new research groups, societies and publications, it has been fostered by a relatively small number of people. Meanwhile, the vast majority of each profession remains either completely indifferent or, at best, only vaguely interested.

This may be inevitable in a period when greater specialization has brought about an undeniable improvement in basic, technical competence, but on the other hand the unnatural divorce of the two disciplines has destroyed the possibility of cross-fertilization and introduced a blinkered view of the nature of historical evidence. The opportunities and excitement of a large area of historical experience (as valid a kind of specialization as any other), have been ignored. Those who are now working towards a truly interdisciplinary approach are in reality attempting to graft back to historical studies some of the broader and more co-operative values of the past, when, in spite of many other defects, different kinds of evidence were considered and related. The examples chosen in this chapter are mainly British, not because Britain has a monopoly of these new developments, but because the writer is most familiar with these.

DESERTED MEDIEVAL VILLAGES

One of the best new examples of co-ordination is concerned with the so-called 'deserted medieval village' or DMV, which is not a particularly good or accurate term (in practice sites are studied which are neither deserted, medieval, nor villages).

In 1908 that remarkable field-worker, Hadrian Allcroft, drew attention to extensive earthworks in England which appeared to represent vanished villages.[1] His observation was very acute. 'The characteristic of these sites is the rude rectangularity of the individual foundation-blocks (what we should now call house-platforms) and of the streets, the latter being, as a rule, mere shallow, flat trenches, dividing the area in chequer-fashion, while the foundation-blocks are uniformly raised above the road-levels. No traces of brick or stone are discoverable. . . Where the plough has passed, every trace of the plan will have vanished, but the pottery will remain in abundance.' Allcroft was not the first to notice these sites, (as early as the 18th century county historians like John Bridges of Northamptonshire had remarked on them) but he realized, at a time when very few archaeologists were interested and vaguely ascribed them to such people as Ancient Britons, Danes and Romans, that these sites were part of the medieval and modern settlement pattern which for various reasons had dropped out of use. He saw that the earthworks were to be connected with ancient names still on the map, and with historically-recorded settlements. 'There are very many instances where the entire settlement has died out, leaving perhaps its ancient name attached to some hamlet nearby, to the Hundred, or even to a single farmstead.' He also connected the demise of these settlements with such historical events as the Black Death, the change in the later Middle Ages from arable to pastoral farming, fires and other disasters. This is an excellent example of historical co-ordination, for which Allcroft deserves far more recognition than he has received. Unfortunately his remarks mainly fell on deaf ears, and very few field-workers took up the challenge.

One man who did respond and work on the subject for a limited area, was Canon C. W. Foster. In 1924 he published a list of 149 'extinct villages and other forgotten places' in Lincolnshire.[2] While not all of these were strictly villages (for example, monastic granges were included), this list has served as the basis of work in the area ever since. Like Allcroft, Foster also realized that the earthworks and surviving farms and churches were, in most cases, the remains of decayed villages, whose names were often still on the map. Once a site had been identified with an historical name, it was a logical step to search for documents referring to the place: Foster therefore used sources such as Domesday Book, the Hundred Rolls and printed calendars. Then in the early 1940s, W. G. Hoskins, who has done more than any other scholar of his generation to integrate different kinds of historical evidence, surveyed the lost villages of Leicestershire: he co-ordinated the sites with a much wider range of documents including rentals, hearth-tax returns and parish registers.[3] But in spite of all this pioneer work, it was still possible in 1946 for the distinguished economic historian Sir John Clapham to write that 'deserted villages are singularly rare'.[4]

Since the end of the Second World War, the study of lost villages has developed rapidly. Now, a quarter of a century after Sir John Clapham made his statement, the count of such sites in England and Wales is over 2,000. This development has been associated above all with the name of Maurice Beresford. An economic historian, Beresford realized the advantage of co-ordinating documents with topographical and archaeological research, and carried out detailed work on the lost villages of Warwickshire, Yorkshire and other counties. In 1954 he published his monumental *Lost Villages of England*, which has already been reissued six times. In 1952 he and others founded the Deserted Medieval Village Research Group (DMVRG) which now consists of people drawn from several different academic backgrounds – in particular economic historians, archaeologists, historical geographers and architectural historians.[5] The binding of all interested persons into a group has provided a forum for the exchange of news and views, and has stimulated much new work. Among its varied activities, the DMVRG keeps records, compiles bibliographies for this country and abroad, sponsors excavations and publishes an annual report. Its work is typical of new interdisciplinary groups which are concerned with the co-ordination of different kinds of evidence: if there is to be effective communication and co-operation between people of varied backgrounds, then older societies and journals usually have to be supplemented by new.

One effect of this post-war interest in deserted villages has been to stimulate work of a more general kind outside the immediate province of the DMVRG. For example there is little doubt that recent advances in the identification and dating of Anglo-Saxon and medieval pottery have been partly inspired at least by the Group. Similarly, it has helped to foster a greater interest in documentary sources, particularly those which throw light on the history of population (see pp. 146-8).

It is easy to see why the interests of some historians and some archaeologists converged on the subject of lost villages. As physical sites, lost villages are often obvious features in the landscape, with extensive patterns of banks, ditches, hollow-ways, mounds and platforms. By using his normal methods of field-survey and excavation, the archaeologist can present detailed evidence about the size and form of the settlement, its expansion and shrinkage at different periods, the character of its buildings, and the technology and economy of its inhabitants. On the other hand the historian can adduce abundant documentary evidence for the disappearance of named settlements, for the rise and fall of population at different periods, for changes in farming methods, and in the policies of landlords. What sensitive historian can therefore remain indifferent to those sad and haunted places, and what sensitive archaeologist can remain indifferent to those informative documents? Sooner or later the appearance of a co-ordinated specialization was inevitable, with historians and archaeologists working side by side, learning from one another and trying to understand the implications of the total evidence. Much work in this field has in fact been done by scholars working in pairs: for example Beresford and Hurst, Hilton and Rahtz.

In 1953, soon after its foundation, the DMVRG took over the systematic excavation of a deserted village, with the eventual

aim of total excavation. The site chosen was Wharram Percy
in a picturesque, steep valley of the Yorkshire Wolds. It has
good earthworks covering a large area; the only upstanding
buildings are the ruinous church and a pair of 19th-century
cottages. Excavation of such a complicated site is a slow,
painstaking business: after 20 seasons only a few relatively
small areas had been excavated.[6] This is partly because the
structural history of each house is proving very complicated,
owing to frequent modification and rebuilding. For example,
a stone house of the 15th century (known as House 6) shows
three building phases – a major modification every generation
or so. In addition, houses are sandwiched on top of one another
and have different sizes and orientations: in area 10 there were
at least seven major phases, ranging from a 12th-century stone-
built manor house to five successive houses of the 14th and
15th centuries parallel to the street, and three at right angles.
Highly complicated patterns of post-holes, stake-holes, hearths
and charcoal flecks, as well as walls and ditches, have to be
carefully excavated, recorded, and interpreted as successive
structures.

The entry in Domesday Book and the place-name leave
no doubt that a pre-conquest community did exist, though
not necessarily on the same site (as archaeologists rightly
observe). It is very likely that the main part of the original
village lay on the lower terrace of the valley near the church,
but as this is an area whose height was increased in medieval
times by eight or ten feet, it will be difficult and costly to dig.
In this vicinity, 8th-century grass-tempered pottery has been
found, and in the churchyard a Northumbrian silver coin of
c.750 which suggests that Wharram was older than the secondary Viking settlement implied in the usual interpretation
of the place-name. In 1965 the excavators tentatively claimed
that, 'there seems to be a good chance that there was already
a burying place and perhaps a church at Wharram in the 8th
century'; in 1969 this view was strengthened by the discovery
(under the south aisle of the church) of a fragment of a late
8th- or early-9th-century cross. However the best evidence of
the antiquity of the village on the lower part of its present site
comes from under the church itself.

For St Martin's church, architectural historians had already
worked out, from the evidence standing above-ground, a
complicated structural evolution from Norman times onwards.

But since 1963, excavation has proved the existence of at least
nine structural periods *below*-ground.[7] The earliest building
consists of foundation trenches cut into natural chalk with a
3-foot-wide wall above, forming a nave 30 feet long and 15
feet wide internally, and a chancel 9 feet square. As yet no
conclusive dating evidence has been found, but, because another larger Saxon building was recognized in 1970 under the
Norman walls, it is possible that the earliest building is pre-
Danish (i.e. 9th-century or earlier).

This work, architectural and excavational, is distinguished
for two reasons: it is the most detailed analysis ever done for
an English parish church, and it is securely part of a wider
study involving the whole village. In the first respect, it con-
tinues and deepens the work of generations of ecclesiologists,
and makes the church more significant both as a building and
as an institution. In the second respect, the work at Wharram
surely points the way ahead to a much fuller use of parish
churches as part of the physical fabric of villages. The church
is one of the most stable elements in the local landscape: not
only is it usually the oldest surviving building of the village,
but it is frequently the youngest of a series of buildings on the
same site. Even where the village has moved or completely
perished, the church very often remains to indicate its site.
Yet in spite of its antiquity, it must never be forgotten that
the site of the church not infrequently appears to be a late
addition to the plan of its village – not really surprising, for
most parishes were created in late Anglo-Saxon and medieval
times to serve pre-existing communities.

It is important to remember that many early documents
deal, not with villages as such but with larger ecclesiastical or
secular units like the parish, tithing, vill or manor. Because
these units *can* change in shape and size, we are not always
able to tell what precise area a document is referring to. A
further complication arises from the fact that parishes frequently contain more than one centre of population, so that
any lists or counts of inhabitants cannot be simply equated
with the main village alone. In the case of Wharram Percy,
for example, the parish also contained three hamlets which
have become depopulated and the now-separate village of
Thixendale.

Where documents refer to individual buildings, it may be
possible to identify them with archaeological sites. Beresford,

for example, has suggested that one rather unusual group of earthworks at the north end of Wharram Percy village (a large enclosure which seems to contain a many-roomed building) may well be *unum capitale messuagium in quo edificatur una grangia* mentioned in an Inquisition of 1368.[8] When the site is completely excavated, and perhaps found to be an unusually large and sophisticated building compared with the rest of the village, then its identification as a manor-house or capital messuage will be more certain – though even then, of course, not absolutely proven. Obviously the identification of sites with documentary references is most likely where the building is of an unusual and distinctive form (such as a manor-house, a water-mill, a dovecot, or a church) or where the documentary reference contains detailed abuttals that can still be recognized.[9] By contrast, it is unlikely that the 'messuage formerly in the tenure of Reynold Martynson', also mentioned in the Inquisition of 1368, will ever be identified with an earthwork or an excavated building because it is presumably just one of a common type in the village street. Most of the medieval references to the village give no more than an impression of *overall* size (for example, there were 16 messuages mentioned in a survey of 1436). Only when a site like Wharram Percy is totally excavated shall we know how far the two kinds of evidence tie up at different dates: the pattern of surface earthworks is strictly evidence for the period when the last inhabitants were evicted, in this case about 1510, and it is the buried layers against which medieval references will have to be measured.

SHRINKAGE OF SETTLEMENTS

Of course lost villages are not the only aspect of rural settlement which is now attracting attention. The definition of a 'deserted medieval village' is necessarily arbitrary: the DMVRG has itself suggested 'any site with evidence of former village status but now possessing only a farm and/or manor (with or without a church and parsonage)'. But however one defines the term, lost villages are best regarded as one end of a long spectrum. We have come to realize that many rural settlements, while not entirely or substantially deserted, are to various degrees depleted. Sometimes the existence of earthworks, empty plots (or tofts), and ruinous buildings shows that a village is only a fraction of its former size, but in other less pronounced cases a few gaps where houses once stood may be all that is visible. Archaeologists, historical geographers and others are now showing more interest in the shrinkage of settlements, and in relating it to population trends and economic history – which clearly means the combination of physical and documentary evidence.

A good example, published in 1965, is a study by Margaret Spufford of the Cambridgeshire parish of Chippenham.[10] Her object was 'to trace the effect of the rise and fall of population on landholding, and so on the physical layout of the village and its fields'. By studying documents such as Domesday Book, Poll Tax returns of 1377, a manorial survey of 1544, and a map of 1712, Mrs Spufford was able to plot the physical effect of the Black Death and its aftermath: the built-up area of the village shrank by over half, as the furthest crofts and streets were abandoned, and gaps appeared in the main village street itself. At the end of the 17th century, the creation of a large park around the house of Edward Russell, later Lord Orford, destroyed the southern half of the main village-street, and the remainder was converted into a model or estate village. The effect of these and other historical changes was that Chippenham as shown on a map of 1712 was 'the skeleton of a community which had once been three times the size'.

In studies of this kind the physical evidence is more usually thought of as topographical rather than archaeological, because it is largely above-ground. Mrs Spufford has related her documentary evidence to the general shape of the village and parish – that is, the lay-out of streets, crofts, buildings, park and fields – which is either visible today or can be restored by the use of maps. Little archaeological work of the normal kind has been done: there are extensive earthworks representing streets, houses and tofts at the southern end of the original village, which should ultimately be surveyed and excavated, and a determined search elsewhere in the parish could well produce scatters of pottery, earthworks and cropmarks. In other words, only a part of the total archaeology of the place has so far been studied.

The phenomenon of shrinkage makes us realize an important characteristic of all living settlements – that they are rarely static. In response to population trends and various social and economic pressures they are constantly modifying their physical character by expansion, contraction, maintenance, decay or redevelopment. Recent field-work has shown that a nucleated village can in the course of time become loose-knit and fragmented, and *vice versa*. Furthermore villages frequently shift their sites entirely. Even when there is apparent stability the same village can at different times have contracted and expanded, so that the tide of settlement may have swept back and forth several times over the same ground. Only careful work on both the physical and documentary evidence will reveal what has happened, how and why. As more is found out about rural communities by field-work, excavation and documentary research, the changes that time can bring will be better appreciated. There may indeed be striking physical stability and continuity, but we should never assume it.

URBAN HISTORY

The most complicated form of human settlement is the town. Urban history is now developing fast, and in an obviously interdisciplinary way. Historians of different kinds, archaeologists, geographers, sociologists, architects, economists and others are increasingly fascinated by town-life, which is of course the way in which the vast majority of people have to live in modern industrial society. Sources of information include a great range of public and private documents, maps and prints, buildings, the topographical pattern of streets, open spaces, defences and boundaries, and buried features recovered by excavation. Because towns are highly complex social and physical phenomena, the compulsion to step over disciplinary boundaries, to co-operate, and to co-ordinate is perhaps greater than in any other field of history.

As in the case of deserted villages, a group specializing in urban settlement has been formed in Britain. It publishes a newsletter, organizes conferences, and generally provides a focus and forum for all who are interested in the subject.[11] Much of the new work stimulated by this group has an economic and sociological bias, but nevertheless physical evidence is often worked in. For example, H.J. Dyos in his classic study of the growth of the London suburb of Camberwell, was careful to relate social and economic history to the physical background: the lay-out of new streets and properties, the evolving pattern of communications, and the architecture of individual buildings.[12]

In many cases it was historians who first realized the value
of physical evidence in towns. One thinks for example of the
stimulating comments which Maitland made about Cambridge and its growth. Again, scholars such as W. G. Hoskins
and M. W. Beresford have taught us to analyze the topography
of towns, seeing in the physical fabric evidence of historical
events for which sometimes no documents survive. Quite
recently another historian, G. H. Martin, has usefully emphasized
the nature of towns as a physical palimpsest of all periods.
'Historians work with documents, and reach back through
their written and printed text to people . . . The text has a
setting which is ultimately the whole sum of human activity
. . . Communities, like individuals, have their own subtleties,
but so do the places that they inhabit. In some sort a town is
a document; it displays its history in its public faces, as well
as in its archives.'[13]

One of the most detailed studies ever done for an English
town was H. E. Salter's work on Oxford.[14] Steeped in the
documentary history of the place, particularly rich in university
and college archives, he gradually built up a map of the medieval
town. By noting the abuttals given (in charters, rentals, accounts, surveys, etc.) he arranged the properties in a physical
sequence along named streets, often identifying them with
existing sites, boundaries and even buildings. Work of this
kind is the devotion of a lifetime; indeed Dr Salter's work was
unfinished at his death in 1951. Evidence of this sort survives
for many other places, particularly in the institutional archives
of religious houses: for example, Urry has recently reconstructed the physical lay-out of Canterbury in the 12th-13th
century, largely from the archives of the cathedral priory.[15]

Despite much pioneering work by historians, it was not until
after the Second World War that archaeologists began to develop
a serious interest in the total history of towns. True, there
had been plenty of excavations on urban sites long before this
time, but usually the objective had been to recover information
about the pre-medieval history of the place (usually, as far
as English towns were concerned, its Roman phase). The
upper layers representing medieval and later occupation were
not greatly prized: little was known about the pottery and other
artifacts which came from them, and archaeological techniques
were not refined enough to deal with such features as timber-
slots, post-holes, stake-holes, pits and ditches. After the Second

World War, opportunities for excavating large and small areas within European towns increased as a result, firstly of bombing and war-damage, and secondly of redevelopment.

The finest example of large-scale urban archaeology in Britain is surely at Winchester, and particularly associated with the name of Martin Biddle. Since 1949, excavations have been carried out on large and small sites in and around the city. In 1962 the Winchester Excavations Committee was formed to organize a systematic campaign of excavation. Many institutions and bodies have been involved, including universities, local and national societies, government departments, and above all, the local authorities of the city and county. It was realized that at Winchester modern redevelopment gave an unprecedented opportunity for archaeologists to study the history of the town, and that this knowledge would be of abiding interest and value to both inhabitants and visitors. Therefore, provision was made for excavation in advance of redevelopment: an enlightened example which, alas, is not followed by more than a small minority of European cities and towns. During the period 1949-70, more has been learnt about Winchester and its development than for any other major British town: excavations have thrown light on its defences, road-system, public buildings, churches, castle and domestic houses, over periods ranging from the late Iron Age to post-medieval times.

One of the most impressive aspects of the work has been the way in which the excavators have been at pains to relate their archaeological findings to documents. In several of the interim reports, relevant documentary information has been discussed by historians, principally R. N. Quirk and D. Keene. It has proved possible to relate documentary descriptions of buildings and properties with the complicated structures found by excavation. One example, by now very well known, is the identification of the Old Minster founded in the mid-7th century AD by Kenwalh, King of Wessex. Documentary research by the late R. N. Quirk and others had suggested the possibility – even if no more – that the Old Minster originally lay just north of the present cathedral nave. Excavation has now recovered almost the entire plan of an Anglo-Saxon building in this position.[16] For a whole variety of reasons, there is little doubt that this is the Old Minster, and, as the excavator claims, 'the first Anglo-Saxon cathedral to be fully excavated'. Sub-

stantial later modifications to the building are quite consistent
with the work of Bishop Ethelwold who, it is known from
documentary sources, 'strengthened it in its northern and
southern parts with solid *porticus* and divers arches'.[17] In
addition a strong case has been made for the identification of
a pit as the grave of St Swithun, who died *c*. AD 980: this feature
at first lay in a western extension to the original church, on its
main axis, and finally within a 13th- and 14th-century chapel
on the north side of the new cathedral nave. Another large
building to the north of the Old Minster, which has been partially excavated, is thought to be the New Minster, founded
by Edward the Elder and dedicated in AD 903. It is known from
historical sources that the two minsters were so close that
a man could hardly pass between them, that in each choir the
chanting of the other church could be heard, and that the New
Minster lay along the north side of the present cathedral green
and therefore to the north of the Old Minster.

Impressive though these identifications are, the work at
Winchester has involved even more remarkable examples of
co-ordination. It is difficult enough to relate the two kinds of
evidence when one is concerned with major buildings such as
cathedrals and minsters, but it is much more difficult for ordinary
buildings such as domestic houses and shops. One area being
dug in Winchester represents one side of an ordinary medieval
street, and consists of some eleven houses, a row of cottages
and two churches. A highly complex palimpsest of secular
buildings is being patiently stripped year by year: eventually
it is hoped that structures will be found dating from the period
when the present grid of streets was laid out in Anglo-Saxon
times. Side by side with the excavation, detailed documentary
research has been carried out, and it has proved possible to
identify tenements, to trace medieval owners and occupiers,
and to discuss excavated structures in the light of the owner's
occupation and social status. Biddle has claimed 'most satis-
factory and convincing agreement' between the two kinds of
evidence.

The identification of individual properties is based 'on the
abutment of one property on another, usually given in detail
in the documents; on the recorded relationship of certain
properties to easily identifiable points such as St Mary's church
or St Pancras Lane; on fifteenth century surveys with later
amendments; on the descent of each property from owner to

owner until it appears in a deed plan or the earliest edition of
the Ordnance Survey map; and on the coherence of the inter-
locking evidence from all these sources.'[18] This detailed analysis
of the verbal descriptions of various properties is of course
no new thing: this is precisely what Willis and Maitland were
doing in Cambridge in the 19th century, and what Salter was
doing for Oxford in the early 1900s. But its direct association
with the remains of streets and houses, excavated scientifically
and on a significantly large scale, is both new and very important.

One representative example of this work at Winchester must
suffice. From written sources D. Keene has recovered considerable information about a tenement immediately south of
St Mary's church in Lower Brook Street, anciently Tanner
Street. It was held in 1340, and perhaps from the early 13th
century, by the prior and convent of Mottisfont. The tenants
seem to have been fullers. In March 1407 a surviving deed
attests that the tenement was divided into two parts by Richard
and Cecilia Bosynton; they themselves retained the northern
part and granted away the southern. The rooms of the house
are described in some detail, with for example shop and kitchen
on the ground-floor and solar above. As has been said, Lower
Brook Street of today is identifiable by means of documentary
references as the former Tanner Street: this is the basic key on
which all else rests. The street-name, which is said to go back
to Saxon origins, clearly refers to an early tanning industry
which by the later Middle Ages had been replaced or supplemented by cloth-working. The excavators of this street
have found a distinctive building which almost certainly represents St Mary's church, known from documents to have
been abandoned by 1528, and on both sides of it are apparently
secular buildings. The tenement to the south of the church,
which should be Richard Bosynton's, has a physical character
which closely reflects the historical information: for example
it is clearly divided into two halves by a later wall. From its
character and from the archaeological dating, this wall can
be presumed to be the one built by Richard and Cecilia in
March 1407. The tenement which the archaeologists originally,
and for their own recording purposes, called IX/X suddenly
becomes associated with living personalities and precise dates.
Richard Bosynton, who was a fuller and dyer and had in 1380-81
become the Treasurer of the city, lived in this house from at
least 1366. In 1409, only two years after dividing the tenement,

he entered St John's Hospital in Winchester as an aged pensioner. Biddle has described this work as 'tenurial archaeology', a term which aptly expresses its dual nature.[19]

The excavation of Bosynton's tenement has of course provided information about the structural history which was largely ignored by the documents. The building had been modified several times by replacement and extension: for example, the site of house X which was the northern part of the divided tenement had been built on what had originally been an open yard against the church; back rooms had been added subsequent to the front; and the whole frontage of tenements I, IX and X had been rebuilt in a single operation by the end of the 14th century – almost certainly because all three belonged to Mottisfont priory.

The increasing amount of work done on towns by both historians and archaeologists made greater dialogue and co-operation inevitable and highly desirable. There is still a long way to go, but at least a start has been made at Winchester, Southampton, Kings Lynn and elsewhere. In a recent article, Martin Biddle has discussed the problems of combining archaeological and documentary evidence for urban history, and stressed that although it is a difficult task, the rewards are great.[20]   Whereas the documentation is largely of a legal, administrative and financial kind, the archaeological material contains 'the facts of daily life'. By considering the two together, we get a far fuller impression of town life than by an exclusively historical or archaeological treatment. Biddle acknowledges that there is considerable inertia and prejudice to overcome, before the combined approach is generally adopted. There is 'unwillingness on the part of historians to use archaeological evidence, the value of which they felt themselves unable to estimate. Archaeologists on their part often ignore, or uncritically accept, documentary evidence.' The point about uncritical acceptance is a good one: there is a danger that as co-ordination becomes acceptable and even fashionable, we shall be tempted to use the other kind of evidence unthinkingly and automatically.

DEMOGRAPHY

A relatively new kind of documentary history is concerned with population.[21] Although people have been writing on this subject since at least the 1690s when Gregory King compiled his *Observations and conclusions, natural and political, upon the state and condition of England,* demography did not become an historical specialization in Britain and France until after the Second World War. This movement to find out more precise information about population trends in the past has been largely led by economic historians and historical geographers. For the medieval period, work has in the main been concentrated on nationally comprehensive surveys such as Domesday Book, the Hundred Rolls, 1334 Lay Subsidy, 1377 Poll Tax, and 1524-5 Lay Subsidy. These were not compiled of course for demographic purposes, but nevertheless they yield important information on minimum population levels. For the post-medieval period, various fiscal and ecclesiastical surveys are useful, but the most important source, until the decennial censuses begin in 1801, is the parish register. The analysis of registers is a technique first developed in France by Louis Henry, and now widely practised in Britain under the inspiration of the Cambridge Group for the History of Population and Social Structure.

As the purpose of the present book is to explore the interaction of history and archaeology, it is not appropriate here to discuss the details of this new form of documentary history. This has already been attempted in other publications, and in a newsletter published regularly by the Cambridge Group.[22] What is relevant is to point out that population is simply another facet of the study of settlement; in other words, that the figures produced by the demographic historian can be related to the foundation, growth, stability, shrinkage and desertion of human habitations.[23] As population rises, so villages and towns grow in size, houses are extended or subdivided, new houses built over former farmland, and encroachments are made on streets and open spaces. As population declines, so villages and towns tend to shrink in size, houses are abandoned and may become grass-grown earthworks, and properties are often thrown together. As more information about population is found from documents (and demography is now a highly fashionable subject) so it ought to be increasingly co-ordinated with physical evidence of great variety – with buildings, streets, town-plans, buried sites, earthworks, scatters of pottery, and any other relevant features of the landscape. This is something which many local historians in particular need reminding of: very few in England for example think of relating census enumerators' books of the 19th century with tithe maps and awards, and yet the abundant personal details of the one need to be related to the topographical information of the other.

VERNACULAR ARCHITECTURE

Although there were pioneers of vernacular architecture in previous generations, such as C. F. Innocent (*History of English Building Construction*, 1916), S. O. Addy (*The Evolution of the English House* 1898), and N. M. Isham and A. F. Brown (*Early Connecticut Houses,* 1900), architectural historians until a few years ago were mainly concerned with the grander and more sophisticated buildings: understandably so, because churches, castles and stately homes were much more likely to yield a stylistic, dateable framework for the general study of architecture. Now, side by side with the continuing study of the larger buildings and to some extent based on the earlier achievements of men like Rickman and Parker (see pp. 124-5), there is a new emphasis on the rich heritage of small, usually domestic, buildings. Although the aesthetic interest is reduced, their value as common human artifacts which can be studied in the context of social and economic history is immense.

The study of vernacular architecture has undoubtedly been stimulated by the increased pace of destruction. As a result of war, of higher living standards and redevelopment, large numbers of traditional buildings in Europe have been, and are being, swept away. If any historical information is to be derived from them, then clearly a record has to be made before or during demolition. It is ironical that more can be found out about a building while it is being pulled down than at any other time: details of the structure are fully visible, and there is an opportunity to pull away later accretions such as wall-paper and plaster. Paradoxically, although large numbers of buildings have been lost, increasing affluence has also promoted restoration and modernization to an unprecedented degree. This too gives an excellent opportunity for the student to make a record.

To further the study of British domestic buildings, the Vernacular Architecture Group was founded in 1953. Its main activities have been conferences and meetings held in different parts of the country, and the preparation of bibliographies (very necessary because architectural reports are scattered in many historical and archaeological publications).[24] This organization has been extremely effective in keeping the relatively small number of specialists in touch, and in maintaining and raising standards.

The main concern of specialists in vernacular architecture is to analyze the physical fabric of buildings, distinguishing the original elements from those which were added later, and to make a full record by plans, elevations, sections, drawings, photographs and written descriptions. From certain details such as roof-structure, joints and mouldings, it may be possible to assign approximate dates, but this is always a difficult thing to do with relatively unsophisticated buildings. Gradually, too, new methods of scientific dating, such as C14 analysis and dendrochronology, are being introduced to supplement the basically typological approach, and to provide more precise dates. From detailed surveys of limited areas, local types of houses can be recognized with distinctive plans and elevations, their distributions plotted, and some estimate made of the time-span within which they were built. Finally, on the basis of the building methods and materials employed, it is possible to distinguish regional styles of domestic architecture, which often relate to geographical, economic and cultural regions.

The main raw materials of this specialization are of course physical, and they yield information which it is not possible to derive from other sources. But at the same time there is a great wealth of documents which throw light on buildings, their contents, and their use. Scholars such as M. W. Barley and W. G. Hoskins have pointed out the special value of probate inventories, wills, lists of Church property, deeds, surveys and maps. Although they are more prepared to use documents than they were, there is still truth in Hoskins' complaint that 'students of vernacular building, in their zeal for peg-holes, types of roof-trusses, straight joints and so forth, remain woe-fully ignorant of the documentary side of their field of study and seem to be as indifferent to it as the historians are to field-work.' Yet at its best this subject is 'the classical example of a marriage between fieldwork and documents'.[25]

It is important to realize that the records do not in the main describe buildings as structures; this kind of information is best derived from the buildings themselves. Instead, they enable us to place buildings against a human background, and to relate them to the social and economic history of which they form part. One learns, for example, of the wealth and possessions of owners and occupiers, of their social status, of the number of inhabitants (family and servants), and of the uses and furnishings of individual rooms. Even probate inventories are not concerned with houses as such, but are legal surveys of the possessions of a deceased person, as left in the rooms and outbuildings of a house.

In general it is quite difficult to relate a surviving house with documents which refer specifically to its history. This is because addresses in the modern sense were not used until a few generations ago. Instead, houses were usually named after their owners or former owners, and therefore in the course of their history they may have changed name several times. Co-ordination is perhaps easiest where a building has had a communal or semi-public significance – for example, manor-houses, parsonages, inns, and charity houses – because it is either physically distinctive or the tradition of its former use survives.[26] But even if it proves impossible to relate documents to a particular building, they are still valuable as background evidence of general categories of house, and the kinds of people who occupied them.

In 1970, S. E. Rigold usefully defined three categories of dating evidence for vernacular buildings.[27] 'Integral' evidence occurs when some indication of a date is attached to a building: it may be an inscription (with or without an actual date), or some kind of personal or family symbol (heraldry, merchant's mark, badge or rebus, or a representational embellishment (for example, a human figure with recognizable costume). Most of these only give a date-bracket of varying width, and all can only strictly relate to that *part* of the building to which they are attached. Furthermore, inscriptions must be treated critically in order to find out their true relationship to the architectural features that carry them: for example they commonly refer, not to the original erection of a building, but to a subsequent change of ownership or period of restoration. 'Circumstantial' evidence is documentation which does not specify the actual building, but which describes historical events that are probably connected with it: fires or road-widening which necessitated rebuilding in a town, or the foundation of certain institutions like colleges and gilds, or even a change of ownership for a particular estate or property, are cases in point. Finally, 'contingent' evidence is the best kind of documentation which implies that work was specifically undertaken at an identifiable place (e.g. accounts, chronicles and building contracts). Even here, however, there is no absolute certainty that the present structure is the one specified in the document (this problem was discussed at length on pp. 102-5, using the example of Ely cathedral).

A piece of research carried out in a Suffolk parish, in which the writer was involved, provides a typical illustration of the methods of co-ordinating small buildings and documents, and the problems encountered. A written survey of the parish of Walsham-le-Willows in 1695 seemed to compare very closely with the earliest surviving map, made in 1817. Starting from easily-identifiable points like road junctions, it could be shown that most fields and properties retained their name and form between those two dates; in fact this has been a very stable landscape until the hedge-clearing of recent years. From a detailed comparison of these sources, it seemed that the tenement of John Salkeld in 1695 was the farm now known as the Woodlands. The deeds of the property, subsequently produced by the owner, proved the association, for they were a continuous series going back to the time of the Salkeld family.[28] Fortunately also, the Woodlands has not been subsequently rebuilt, and appears typologically to be a three-celled building of the early 17th century which had been subsequently extended by the addition of a wing at right angles. The inventory compiled on the death of Salkeld in 1699 agrees very closely with the present house. Most of the rooms can be easily identified, and the number of fireplaces in the three impressive chimney-stacks agrees with the andirons, dogs, tongs, spits and other pieces of hearth equipment. The house was obviously comfortably furnished, as befitted the residence of a clergyman and former Fellow of Queens' College, Cambridge. His 'Librah of Bookes' worth £30 is certainly not the kind of thing one normally expects in Suffolk farmhouses at this period!

Salkeld was an interesting cleric of presbyterian persuasion, who had been expelled at the Restoration from his rectory at Worlington.[29] He came to live at Walsham, but not in total retirement. In 1672 he was licensed to hold presbyterian services at his house (this may have been the occasion for putting a new doorway in the northern wing, giving access to a room, now the kitchen, which would have been suitable for meetings). In addition he was still preaching occasionally in local parish churches, and was imprisoned at least twice for his outspoken opinions on the Restoration church. On his death in 1699 he left a modest estate with property in Walsham and four other Suffolk parishes.

Once a surviving building has been connected with a tenement named in an historical document, and with an historical person, then several other documents and pieces of information may fall easily into place. In the case of Salkeld, his admission to his lands, as well as their surrender on his death, can be found recorded in the court books of Walsham manor. His will, proved on 20th March, 1699/1700, also survives in the records of the Archdeaconry of Sudbury. Furthermore, because former owners of tenements are usually named in manorial records, it is possible to trace later and earlier occupiers of the same property. It was found that Salkeld received the copyhold in 1664 on the surrender of one Thomas Rampley, gentleman. Yet in the 1695 survey, the tenement is described as sometime of *Richard* Rampley. In fact, an earlier survey of 1581, now kept in Chicago, shows that this Richard Rampley was the occupier in Elizabethan times, almost a century earlier. Before him again, it belonged to one Ralph Stokes. And so it is possible to build up a chain of ownership going back to the middle of the 16th century. It is likely that the house we see today was built very largely in the time of the Rampley family, soon after 1600, and stylistically the north wing cannot be much later. This kind of study is essentially the same as Biddle's 'tenurial archaeology'; all the while one is trying to interpret buildings in terms of human lives and decisions.

There is one other dimension to the story of the Woodlands which is relevant here. At the northeast corner of the house, where the two wings touch, there is a small section which seems to be the relic of an earlier building. It has an impressive truss which now runs axially with the main range, but which originally seems to have formed part of a house at right-angles. Stylistically 16th-century, it could have been the rebuilt parlour-end of an earlier, probably medieval, house. As the Woodlands is along a length of street where it is known from documentary evidence that medieval tenements stood, and where medieval pottery has been found, it seems highly likely that it is on a medieval site. Though it is impossible to prove continuity, it is also interesting that the owner has recently turned up a quantity of Roman pottery in the stackyard behind the house, including an apparent cinerary urn. This is certainly a good habitation site, immediately beside a stream, and it is likely to have been occupied continuously long before John Salkeld retired there in about 1662.[30]

INDUSTRIAL ARCHAEOLOGY

This term seems to have been coined by Michael Rix in 1955,[31] and has been defined as the study 'of physical remains of industry in the past', particularly of the so-called Industrial Revolution which began some 200 years ago. These physical remains include many kinds of building and structure, such as mills, factories, warehouses, furnaces, kilns, canals and bridges. Most can be studied, even if ruinous, as surface remains, though sometimes excavations are carried out. Since 1955 an increasing number of books and articles on the subject has been published, and a new specialist journal was founded in 1964.[32] In most parts of Britain, societies, groups and individuals are taking up the challenge of recording industrial sites before they are altered or destroyed. Indeed one of the main stimuli has been the deliberate reclamation and redevelopment of derelict industrial sites, as an act of public policy.

Again, we should not make the mistake of assuming that the subject did not exist before the 1950s, even though the current name had not been invented. For example, the Newcomen Society, with a largely engineering bias, has been working in this field since its foundation in 1919, and its Transactions first appeared in 1922. Even in the 19th century there were individuals who carefully described industrial sites and processes: one, H. S. Cowper, in his superb history of Hawkshead parish in Lancashire (1899), was much concerned with the local iron industry and various woodland crafts from medieval times onwards.

There can be no possible objection to the use of the word *archaeology* in this connection. A blast-furnace or a cotton-mill or a bridge is as much physical evidence from the past as a bronze spearhead or cinerary urn. But as it is part of relatively modern history, this is a subject where the study of plentiful physical remains can, and must, be combined with a wealth of documents – company records, parliamentary papers and

acts, commercial directories, sale catalogues, and Ordnance
Survey maps and the like. The general identification of an
industrial site is usually easy. Even a derelict factory or mill
usually retains a name, or is marked and named on an early
map, and local people often remember the processes that went
on. In addition, some structures and machines are 'documents'
in their own right, bearing the names of makers and their place
of manufacture. The great opportunity of the subject lies in
the attempt to correlate the industrial landscape of buildings,
structures and machines with the more personal, social and
economic considerations which are revealed in detailed records: the enterprise and inventiveness of individuals, conditions of work, the nature of various occupations, and so on.

It is also worth pointing out that historical evidence of the
non-written or oral kind is particularly valuable in this field.
When for example old people are talking about their former
crafts and occupations, and particularly in front of surviving
machines and tools, then they can give remarkably detailed
evidence which would unobtainable from any other source.

So far the number of studies fully combining both kinds of
evidence is small. Very little of the vast wealth of documentary
sources has yet been used by industrial archaeologists, whose
main interest is often in physical technicalities alone. In a
way it seems strange and sad that a new specialization had to
appear – surely an awareness of the physical evidence still
littering the landscape ought to have developed in the minds
of economic historians working on the Industrial Revolution?
But no: except in a few cases, economic historians have not
shown much interest, and so the archaeology of the Industrial
Revolution was discovered and developed by engineers, architects, local historians and others. One hopes that the present
division into industrial archaeology and industrial history will
disappear as the two groups grow into one another and merge
their identity.

HISTORICAL ECOLOGY
As a final example of the interdisciplinary trends of recent
years, involving both physical and written evidence, it is worth
mentioning the increasing contact between the worlds of history
and botany. The raw material of botanical studies is of course
plant-life, but like any other kind of physical evidence plants

can be of interest historically. They can be evidence either of
the natural environment in which man found himself in the
past, or more likely they can be a measure of the way in which
the environment has been modified by a great variety of human
activities.

Most of the botanical evidence which has been studied by
palaeobotanists and borrowed by archaeologists, is fossil-
like in nature: it consists of plant-remains which no longer
survive in their natural and original environment, but have
been freakishly preserved in certain natural or archaeological
contexts. For example work on cereal grains found on archaeological sites has indicated how cultivated cereals were
gradually bred out of wild grasses. The study of pollen grains
sampled from layers of mud in lakes and fens has revealed the
nature of natural vegetation at different periods in the past,
and has sometimes suggested nearby cultivation of cereals.
For historical periods, the evidence of botany is no less valuable.
For instance, dendrochronology which is a means of dating
timber absolutely by counting and correlating tree-rings, is of
great potential for architectural historians, and to a lesser
extent for medieval archaeologists. The fact that it is possible
to correlate this method with C14 dating adds very appreciably
to its value.

A *living* specimen may also have an historical significance.
Archaeologists in North America, Greenland and other parts
of the world have shown how buried sites determine the flora
growing on them, and how therefore certain plants can be used
to find new sites.[33] The crop-mark, indicating the differential
growth of crops because of buried features, is a well-known
principle in archaeological field-work. Finally, living plants
may even have a limited chronological significance: a fine
lofty oak now grows in the ruinous nave of East Somerton
parish church (Norfolk): if ever that tree were felled, a count
of its annual rings would afford the minimum period of abandonment since the church was last used as a *barn* (in the south
wall is the opening of a barn door). Even without felling, a
qualified person could give some estimate of the tree's age.
This kind of evidence could be a particularly useful guide for
industrial archaeologists, as many of their sites are now choked
with vegetation.

Furthermore, many botanical specimens can be shown to
be, in a very real sense, humanly-made artifacts. The peculiar,

knobbly shape of a pollard, caused by the deliberate and systematic cutting of branches from the top of the trunk, is a
good example: this is the result of local people exercising common and tenancy rights, and lopping timber for fuel and other
purposes. Nor need the point be confined to individual specimens: whole areas containing thousands of plants can equally
well be regarded as artifacts. For example, many woods all
over England were regularly coppiced from the Middle Ages
down to within living memory, and in a few places the practice
still survives today. This means that certain shrubs and trees,
such as hazel, ash and hornbeam, were regularly cut down at
ground level, encouraging the growth of multiple shoots in
clumps or 'stools'. The shoots grew into stems of various sizes,
which were harvested in strict rotation and could be used in a
variety of local industries, such as the making of hurdles, fences,
gates, and tool-handles, or even as rafters and studs in local
buildings. Many of the surviving English woods are derelict
coppices (copses), and the great hollow stools, particularly
of ash, are themselves physical evidence of careful human
management in the past.[34] The same point could be applied
to much larger areas such as the fells of the Pennines and Lake
District, and the moorland of Devon and Cornwall, which
have been moulded and modified by various human activities:
the felling of trees, early arable farming on former forest soils,
and the introduction of systematic animal grazing. In other
words, the present vegetational cover is not simply the result
of natural factors such as altitude, soils and climate, but has
also been affected by numerous human decisions in the past.

And so the interests of botanists and certain representatives
of the historical world have tended to converge. Already in
Britain an Historical Ecology Group has been set up by officers
of the Nature Conservancy. Although the initiative has come
from the scientific side, the group now includes historians (whose
main interests are in the local, topographical, agricultural and
economic fields), historical geographers and archaeologists.
The main activities are lectures and conferences to explore
the interaction and overlapping of three kinds of evidence:
the physical evidence of botany, the physical evidence of archaeology, and the documentary evidence of history.

There are many historical sources which could be coordi-
nated with botanical evidence, mainly those already widely
used for their own purposes by economic, agrarian and local

historians. Among the more obvious are surveys, maps, enclosure records, accounts, sale catalogues, deeds and legal depositions. These and many others describe a variety of human activities which are likely to effect plant-life, such as the techniques of arable and pastoral farming, drainage, the management of hedges and woodland, and the development of local industries. Yet in spite of the potentialities, very few people have made systematic use of this material and combined it with botanical research. One good example which points the way ahead is the co-operation of W. G. Hoskins, the economic and topographical historian, with Max Hooper, a botanist of the Nature Conservancy.[35] Hooper, believing with others that the older the hedge the more species of tree and shrub it tends to have, has developed the theory that each major species represents approximately one hundred years of the hedge's life. The dates obtained by counting species over lengths of thirty yards were compared with those provided by Hoskins from various historical sources, and in a significantly high proportion of cases they agreed. It is important to remember that the individual plants are not immortal, but that in a plant-community like a hedge, trees and shrubs, once deliberately or accidentally introduced, tend to regenerate and maintain themselves. Precisely why old hedges tend to be rich botanically is not fully understood, and there is little doubt that important qualifications will be made to Hooper's theory as more fieldwork is carried out. Nevertheless, this theory and method is clearly of great importance to all these interested in landscape history, and it represents the kind of co-operation which deepens the knowledge of all concerned. By such projects the archaeologist-historian will have a much fuller appreciation of the physical character of many landscape features while the botanist is better able to come to terms with the dimension of time and the effects of human actions.

In case this discussion of co-ordination gives the impression that there is no substance in earlier complaints about infrequent contact between archaeology and history, one vital distinction should be reiterated. Co-ordination has indeed been practised for centuries and is still developing, but it only concerns a small minority relative to the total number of researching and teaching members of each profession. In addition, as has been said, very little systematic teaching of the co-ordinated approach is provided. It is therefore the stimulus of actual research which has led to most new developments, and not the discipline of intellectual training. Finally and worst of all, behind the particular problems of relating words and things, there lies the aggressive ignorance and lack of interest which so many members of either profession still display towards the other. While it is perfectly understandable that everyone does not want to use both kinds of evidence at research level, the general lack of interest is quite unforgivable. We have reached a curious stage in historiography where a necessary refinement of techniques, begun in the 19th century, has only gone so far, and at the moment is actively discouraging methodological experiment and the thinking-out of a practical philosophy which covers all kinds of historical evidence.

7 An appeal for total archaeology

This final chapter is an appeal for the widest possible application of archaeology and its methods, so that it covers the entire physical environment of a given area. This follows logically from the definition offered earlier, that archaeology comprises all kinds of physical evidence, of all dates. It would seem a very obvious thing in view of the modern prehistorian's increasing interest in environment and ecology, for some archaeologists to expand this approach into the complete study of given landscapes – their original natural state, and their gradual colonization and exploitation by man from prehistory down to the present day. It does not matter whether this kind of archaeology is called 'total', stressing the fullness of the physical evidence, or 'local', stressing the inevitably tight geographical limits, as long as it is realized that these characteristics go together. It is not suggested that archaeology should abandon its traditional concentration on periods, cultures and kinds of artifact, but that this should be supplemented by a parallel emphasis on full landscape history.

One great advantage of total archaeology is the opportunity it affords of widespread co-ordination with documentary evidence. Documents can be enormously informative about the environment, providing much more detail about human needs, motives and methods than is normally deduced from physical evidence alone. Indeed total archaeology as a new approach is clearly stimulated by the development in recent years of local history, and particularly by the way in which local historians have deliberately emphasized *place* as the setting of, and influence on, human life in the past. The founders of the modern school of local history have repeatedly stressed that 'the study of topography is the foundation of local history'.[1]

The purpose of the 'total' approach is to study a section of the landscape as fully as possible. First, this means that (against normal archaeological practice) the total archaeologist will attempt to explain all the *living* features which are in use to-day, for example inhabited buildings, hedge-patterns and the road-system. Secondly, he will study all the usual *fossil* or dead features: the things which are still discernible, but no longer of any real social or economic significance (crop-marks, soil-marks, earthworks, ruinous buildings and so on). They can be fragments of completely different early landscapes which for a variety of reasons show through the modern pattern, or they can be early elements of the existing landscape which are now abandoned.

In most areas there will be found physical evidence for four main aspects of economic life. First, there is the pattern of human settlement, or the way in which at different periods man chose, or was forced, to live in relation to his fellows and in relation to the natural landscape. This involves all kinds of human habitation, both individually and in the groups which they form (ranging from isolated houses and farms, through hamlets and villages, to towns and vast conurbations). Secondly, there is the pattern of communications (e.g. paths, roads, canals, railways, air-fields) which man developed partly at any rate under the influence of natural factors. Thirdly, there is the evidence for food-production and land-use in the form of living or buried vegetation, lynchets, fields, hedges, walls, ditches, commons, woods, buried pollen and so on. Fourthly, there is the evidence for commercial and industrial activity (other than agriculture) such as quarries, mines, shops, markets, inns, kilns, mills, factories and the natural geology. These four categories by no means exhaust the range of physical evidence: there are temples, churches and funerary monuments to remind us of the religious instinct; amphitheatres, cock-pits and football-grounds, reflecting the human need for re-creation and amusement; town-halls, prisons and triumphal arches, representing the eternal problems of government and politics; and so on. These are often no more than the physical tokens of the complex social life led by man as the most gre-garious and highly-organized of animals, and usually they do not of themselves lead to secure historical interpretations. All the features mentioned above form the 'total archaeology', the unique blend of physical characteristics, of any one area.[2]

There is, however, one aspect of economic life which, though not easy to recover from physical evidence alone, is a primary objective for the modern ecologically-minded archaeologist: he must always be looking for the economic 'territory' which belongs to every human unit, and the boundaries (simple or complex) which define it. This is clearly a blend between settlement-history and land-use, and ranges from the seasonal hunting-grounds of primitive nomads and the territory of an individual house or farm, through larger estates and social groups (such as the medieval manor and parish) to the higher economic units (such as the areas served by large towns or ports). Often economic territories will coincide with administrative units (secular and ecclesiastical), and boundaries, once established, can influence subsequent economic decisions: this is why the full study of territories and boundaries is best done by the co-ordination of physical and documentary evidence.

It may be objected that this approach is against the trend towards greater specialization. As more work is done and more knowledge accumulates, some will say that it is impossible for a single individual to master more than one main period. Admittedly there are limits to what one person can do, but the finding of a viable specialization has always been a question of juggling with chronological *and* geographical limits, according to the amount of evidence available. Though most people until now have chosen to work on subjects with a comparatively restricted time-span but wide geographical scope, it is also possible to study the complete archaeological history of a quite small area. This is frequently done for instance by museum curators, who for a limited area have to be capable of assessing sites and finds ranging from prehistoric to modern. Obviously, to do this well, they should also possess broad background knowledge and be in touch with those who specialize in periods, cultures or artifacts.

Total archaeology, though, is an even more intensive study. For example in Britain, C. C. Taylor has recently concerned himself with a single parish, Peter Fowler with a block of chalk downland, and Barry Cunliffe with an area of 20 square miles (see pp. 170-5). Within such relatively small geographical limits, one is concerned with every physical feature which throws light on the interaction of man and a particular environment. This essentially localized approach can be justified in the same way as Hoskins, Finberg and others have justified the modern school of local history. The local study is not simply a microcosm of the larger national scene: it has validity in its own right, because this is the setting against which distinctive communities have lived and died over generations. Admittedly there is always the danger of becoming far too 'parochial', and of forgetting the larger world outside, but this is a danger which must be faced at any level – local, national or continental. In the mind of any student there must be constant interaction between the particular and general, and between his own chosen study and the world outside. Even so, the work is still to some extent selective – although one hopes to survey every feature of interest, down to minor earthworks and small scatters of pottery, one certainly cannot excavate them all, nor can one fully record every building and consult every extant document. But in adopting this approach one has the consolation of studying man and his environment in a much fuller way than is normally possible. The locality as a whole becomes an artifact, created by man and nature over centuries and millennia: the history of each individual feature contributes to the larger history of the area, and *vice versa*. This is a view which some prehistorians are already backing, when in spite of the opposite trend towards more meticulous and detailed excavation they also recommend the survey of areas rather than individual sites.[3] The concern with a locality, and with a distinctive local way of life, is one of the basic realities of human existence at all periods; to ignore this is to dehumanize the study of archaeology. As Peter Fowler has wittily put it: 'after all what worried Joe Celt was not whether he was conforming to the La Tène III norm or producing enough artifacts for statistical analysis but whether the spring would dry up this year, whether he could push his fields further into the woods, or whether his feckless neighbour at Dindun was going to curb his pyromania these coming winter nights.'[4]

Admittedly, this subject could be called 'historical geography', 'topographical history', 'human ecology' or 'landscape history', as readily as 'total archaeology'. These terms do not mean a great deal, except that they stress the background and training of various groups whose interests converge on landscape history. Specifically, historical geography is a fast-developing specialization where geographers combine their observation of physical elements in the landscape with the study of historical documents. In fact the competence displayed in historical techniques can be very impressive, giving the lie to some professional historians who believe that theirs is a deep mystery which cannot be penetrated by outsiders. Yet historical geography has its weaknesses. It often works on a scale which is too small to bring out the full significance of its evidence, surveying regions rather than individual communities – often because of an understandable desire to express information cartographically. There is also a tendency to rely too much on chronological cross-sections based on outstanding documents: in England, for example, there are the almost magical dates of 1086, 1334, 1371 and 1524-5, dependent on the comprehensive surveys of Domesday Book and later tax assessments. Finally, although geographers also specialize in physical evidence and are skilled in describing present patterns, they are not always so good in tracing origins and changes. There is a curious tendency to accept, rather uncritically, present patterns as old and original – the prime example is the ancient geographical sport of classifying village-plans, now shown by archaeological fieldwork to be totally inadequate as a means of historical description and analysis: villages have frequently changed shape, size and even site. It is because of such weaknesses in the historical use of physical evidence that the expertise of the archaeologist is urgently needed. If only more archaeologists would concentrate on limited geographical areas, and learn the related techniques of documentary research, great strides could be made in the understanding of man's relationship with his environment.

One very real justification for this approach is that it avoids the wasteful and myopically specialized work that so many archaeologists indulge in. With their interest set on one period, or on one kind of site, they survey extensive areas and dismiss masses of physical evidence which is irrelevant to their main purpose. The present writer must confess that he has surveyed many areas in the North of England in exactly that way – looking for relatively isolated features such as Roman roads, barrows and scatters of Mesolithic flints, but not trying to understand the area as a whole. While the majority of archaeologists will no doubt (and rightly) continue to specialize in a chronological period, it is to be hoped that a growing number will taste the great satisfaction of studying the complete archaeology of relatively small areas. In fact, cultural and local archaeology need one another because each provides an intensity and emphasis which the other lacks; local archaeology cuts across the traditional forms of archaeological specialization, and in so doing, strengthens and is strengthened.

SOME ARCHAEOLOGICAL ATTITUDES

Archaeologists have traditionally been concerned with pre-history and early historic times, and they have not yet come to terms with the full implications of studying later periods. All the same, the growing general interest in Europe for medieval, post-medieval and industrial archaeology, and in America for colonial and 'historical' archaeology, must impinge on those who think about the methods and character of the subject, and make the acceptance of the 'total' approach more likely.[5] After all, features of the present, living landscape, such as certain hedges and ditches, turn out to be quite early in date, and they are therefore contemporary with or earlier than the villages, moats, churches, cemeteries, and towns which are now being assiduously excavated. For some extra-ordinary reason, archaeologists (unlike their specialist cousins, the architectural historians) have been reluctant to study land-scape features which are upstanding and still in use. But the date of any humanly-made artifact or landscape feature should not exclude it from consideration: the essential point is that it was designed and made by human beings in the past, for particular social and economic reasons. If it is still in use, so much the better because it will be comparatively well-preserved in a living context, and may be documented also. After all, there is no essential difference between the lynchets and banks of prehistoric fields and 19th-century enclosure hedges: why should we as archaeologists study the first and ignore the second?

The traditional bias towards the earlier periods of time often means that the upper layers of an excavation are undervalued and recorded inadequately. The way in which a building was destroyed, overlaid and forgotten, and the site used for other purposes, is as interesting historically as the original occupation. Gradually this 'evolutionary' attitude to the past is gaining ground on what one could call the 'purist' or 'simplistic' approach. Witness for example the fascinating controversy over the west front of the medieval abbey at Bury St Edmunds, Suffolk: in the face of considerable local and national pressure, the then Ministry of Public Building and Works had to admit the historical and aesthetic value of 17th- to 19th-century dwellings, built into the craggy ruins of the medieval structure. This enchanting blend of periods stands as evidence for the life of the abbey *and* its secularization since the Reformation.[6] How refreshing it also is to find a growing number of urban archaeologists who are concerned with the entire history of towns – in fact we are probably nearer our objective in the history of certain towns than in many other fields of endeavour.

Professor Cunliffe has recently demonstrated in a vivid way how buried remains can be integrated with living, surface features. At Idsworth, Hampshire, he obtained permission to excavate around an inhabited house called Manor Farm, which dates mainly from the 15th-16th century but has an earlier core. He found the remains of a 13th-century aisled hall of which the existing house was clearly a fragment, subsequently extended. Furthermore, under this building was another aisled hall at right angles to the first. Here of course any distinction between archaeology and architectural history, or between excavation and survey, is of minor importance: both kinds of physical evidence add up to the total history over many centuries of a still-living site. In a sense, the standing house has grown up out of the occupation layers beneath and around: one cannot be fully understood without reference to the other.[7]

The owner of Manor Farm was unusually patient and dedicated, and this sort of excavation cannot be done very often. However, the opportunities which do sometimes occur for excavations around and *under* standing buildings should be seized; as for instance, when a medieval house or church is being restored. The difference in date between a site and the building now standing on it is, or should be, an obvious archaeological objective, for it is of the greatest interest to know how the present structure relates to its predecessors.

Cunliffe's work is an excellent example of the way in which the history of still-living or still-used features can be discovered, and new dimensions added by excavation.[8] In a way this is archaeology of a more impressive kind than the study of dead features like burial mounds and abandoned settlements, because it relates past and present in a continuous, unbroken stream of human life and consciousness.

In the past, the main deterrent to this approach has undoubtedly been the archaeologist's reluctance to come to grips with documentary evidence. While other groups such as historical geographers and ecologists are increasingly familiarizing themselves with historical sources and techniques, relatively few archaeologists have bothered to do so. To follow this approach successfully, one has to be prepared to ignore academic boundaries – certainly the distinctions between archaeology, architectural history, historical geography and documentary history become utterly meaningless, because one needs a working knowledge which embraces them all. In this sense, it is heartening to find Martin Biddle, the excavator of Winchester, saying that in practice he acknowledges no boundary between archaeology and documentary history: to solve the problems he is faced with, he must be ready to use any kind of evidence, and if this means learning the techniques of documentary history he is prepared to do so. But how often does one hear scholars excuse their own lack of enterprise, when they come up against the boundary of another discipline, by saying 'I have no competence in this field'?

Of course the amount of documentary evidence, which could be integrated with the study of total archaeology, is immense. In England it ranges from Anglo-Saxon land-charters to 20th-century sale catalogues, and from Exchequer tax returns to farm-diaries. As well as these 'verbal' sources, there are the more 'pictorial' kinds of evidence in the shape of maps, plans, prints and so on. The sheer bulk and complexity of all this has understandably deterred many people. But once again, it is important to stress that total archaeology can only involve small areas: because the chronological range is wide, and the amount of evidence varied, the geographical limits have to be comparatively narrow. From the work so far done, it is clear that results justify this alternative emphasis.

Some people may say that total archaeology is unnecessary because the history it provides is already known from the study of written documents. If archaeological evidence were merely to tell us what we could get from documents, or simply to illustrate in detail principles derived from documents, it would indeed be a wasteful kind of study. But there is far more to it than that. It certainly overlaps with the knowledge gained from documents, and may be only a subordinate part of the total historical knowledge, but always it provides something extra and distinctive. Take the study of domestic houses from the 16th to 19th centuries: although much can be gained from maps, wills, inventories and title-deeds, we still need to investigate actual buildings for knowledge of what the house was like to look at and live in – its dimensions, raw materials, details of construction, later modifications, and its standards of convenience and comfort. In historical periods, the existence of documents does not make unnecessary the study of physical evidence. On the contrary, the physical evidence is all the more necessary, to answer the problems raised by the documents and *vice versa*. It is one of the peculiar excitements of total archaeology that work in the field alternates with work in the record office or library: one is constantly driven back and forth as the study develops. Archaeologists working on documented periods must at least be in constant dialogue with historians, and make every effort to understand their approach. It is better still for them to learn the use of documents themselves. Historical periods give the archaeologist a chance to study in greater detail and clarity the full range of human decisions which influence the physical environment: surely this is a glorious opportunity for developing archaeology far beyond the uncertainties and ambiguities of the prehistoric past, above all by increasing the available stock of interpretative analogies.

Peter Fowler has rightly said that 'one of the main attractions of local archaeology is that it leads inevitably through history to the present day, and the environment in which the local community now lives.'[9] It is, in other words, a way of explaining the character and individuality of places today, and this should make it of particular value to the general public and modern planners, as they wrestle with the problems of our environment. Planning is now such a varied and far-reaching process that no single person (not even a qualified planner) can hope to be expert in all its aspects. Therefore there is increasing consultation and debate with outsiders who specialize in various environmental subjects – such as architecture, geography, natural history and archaeology. Concerned as he is in the essential physical character of his area, its evolution over centuries and millennia, the total archaeologist must be prepared to give evidence when consulted, and to fight the authorities when he believes mistakes are being made. In the last resort his main function is an educational one. He must convince members of the general public that change is inevitable and has always been so: at the same time he must open their eyes to the unprecedented pace and power of modern technological change, and to the dangers of such change when uncontrolled by intelligence and sensitivity. He must provide evidence that will help to decide which local features are of most value, and therefore worth defending. Take hedges: virtually no attempt has been made in eastern England over the last 20 years to help farmers discriminate between those which ought to have been kept (for example, parish boundaries and the edges of ancient commons) and those which for various reasons are less valuable historically and scientifically. The total archaeologist must hammer away at the difference between genuine local traditions and the suburban values which threaten to swamp everything. In every area, rural and urban, the public are anxious to be told of the historical significance of their surroundings, how for instance the street pattern of a town fossilizes its medieval defences, why several parish boundaries converge at a single point, why a church lies half a mile from its village, and so on. Unfortunately visual awareness is not a common faculty, any more than aesthetic awareness. The total archaeologist therefore has a responsibility, with others, to see that people are concerned and informed about the character, individuality and meaning of the area they live in. Every generation is the temporary trustee of an environment that has evolved over millennia, and will continue to evolve in the future. We have a duty to act as informed and sensitive trustees, who will leave behind physical surroundings which are as distinctive, varied and meaningful as those we inherited, and if possible, more so. 'If any there be which are desirous to be strangers in their owne soile, and forraigners in their owne City, they may so continue and therin flatter themselves.'[10]

CONTINUITY AND CHANGE

There has never been a wholly static landscape, one which over even a short period has remained entirely unchanged. There are always personal, social and economic pressures towards change, as well as various natural processes which have the same effect. Even in the sleepiest rural parishes, farms change hands and 'new brooms' are introduced; buildings are constantly maintained and re-decorated; some people get richer and more acquisitive, while others get poorer; population rises and falls; consolidation, enclosure and subdivision all effect the pattern of farms and fields; some ditches and hedges get neglected, while others are regularly maintained; trees in woodland and hedgerow grow and are felled; natural erosion and deposition are subtly changing the natural contours. Change at times has been slow and small-scale, but it has always been there. This is one reason why modern preservationists and conservationists must never argue for the *status quo*, but for change which is controlled by sensitive and intelligent planning, by the highest standards of design and an awareness of historical roots.

The principle of continuity is just as important. It stresses the antiquity and stability of many physical features. In spite of the tendency towards change, perhaps even because of it, certain basic elements have been allowed to survive for centuries and sometimes millennia – both as fossils and functional objects. It also needs emphasizing that in towns, in spite of the greater pace of change, the factor of continuity is just as important. Take, for instance, the centres of many European towns, which while they have a predominantly 19th-century or modern aspect (as far as their buildings are concerned) still retain a basically medieval street-pattern. In most places it is only in the last 20 years that we have begun to modify ancient street-patterns by massive re-development and the creation of completely new alignments.

There is a common half-way house between continuity and change, which shows how closely related they are. Many a landscape feature is ancient in its form and lay-out, but has been modified over the centuries by use and maintenance. Thus, if the general shape of a village (i.e. its street pattern and property boundaries) has been stable for many centuries, many of its houses will have been rebuilt several times. Humbler features also show the same blend. For example, Dr Raistrick and others have pointed out[11] that while existing dry-stone walls can be over a thousand years old in origin, they have necessarily been repaired and even totally rebuilt in the course of time. Similarly, ditches may have been originally cut centuries ago, but to keep them effective farmers have had to clean and recut them constantly. It is therefore quite possible for the same feature in the course of its history to show both continuity and change.

It so happens that at present these two principles are being pushed by different groups: whereas historians and historical geographers are emphasizing the continuity of many landscape features (for example, the use of sites for settlement and the shape of villages), archaeologists are busily recommending the principle of change (for example, the alteration of property boundaries and the frequent rebuilding and re-siting of houses).

Both are of course right, because, as we have already discussed, change and continuity are each present in the history of any place, and to some extent the different emphasis is the natural result of different kinds of evidence. This makes frequent communication and rapport between specialists all the more necessary; it ensures that in any piece of research the true balance is sought between the two contending principles.

How near are we to total archaeology?

In England of recent years, there have been two outstanding pieces of archaeological field-survey, and both have been claimed as total archaeology.

At Fyfield and Overton Downs, Wiltshire, Peter Fowler attempted to establish the 'land-use history' of an area of about four square miles. With teams of helpers over a period of some 10 years, he has done intensive field-survey of the abundant earthworks which survive on this high downland, and has excavated selected sites.[12] The broader sweep afforded by field-survey is deliberately supplemented in a few places by the more detailed, costly and time-consuming process of excavation. The work has shown how varied and complex a history attaches to one small piece of landscape. As far as settlement was concerned, the main emphasis was understandably on the earlier periods of prehistory and Roman times, when people chose to live and farm at these higher altitudes (as well as in the valleys). Excavation revealed several interesting stratigraphical relationships: for example, on two sites only 400 yards apart, an Iron Age settlement was found *buried beneath* 'Celtic' fields, and a late Roman settlement found *overlying* such fields. Among the sites studied were burial mounds, settlements, fields and lynchets, and a sharpening-bench for stone axes. From medieval times onwards the downland was mainly used for grazing, and to a lesser extent as arable, and belonged to villages and farms in the adjacent valley of the River Kennet. It formed the higher, northern end of strip-like economic and administrative units (tithings, manors and parishes).

Fowler has subsequently admitted that the chalk downland on its own was not an ideal unit of study. It was originally chosen because it abounded in earthworks and was accessible, but not because it was a complete economic unit at any time in the past. Even for prehistoric times it could not be studied in isolation, and 'an early impression was that the Down and activities there were closely related to and perhaps dependent on events and resources in the valley below and the woods beyond.' In spite of the greater difficulties of studying the valley and lowland (because of intensive modern settlement and farming) the patterns of the downland only began to make sense in this wider context. At all periods, the territories of various communities are likely to include a good cross-section of local soils and natural zones – in this case woodland, gravel terraces, water-meadows, a river, gentle valley slopes and chalk downland. It therefore does not make complete historical sense to study any of these in isolation. In England, many parishes are no more than early economic territories taken over for ecclesiastical administration, and are therefore ideal units of study: they are often at least medieval in date, and in some areas may be considerably earlier (Roman or even prehistoric). As Fowler conceded, 'the use of the present parish boundaries to define our area of study was in part justified, or at least as good as any other line.' His speculations about the antiquity of parish and tithing boundaries, about place-names and early land charters, emphasize how total archaeology leads naturally into the field of documentary history, and how the archaeologist is forced, sooner or later, to consider historical concepts.

Fowler has since embarked on an intensive study of the Butcombe area of Somerset. He has chosen to survey an area comprising four parishes. It has a complicated cultural landscape with nucleated villages, hamlets, isolated farms, a tight network of winding roads, and an intricate pattern of fields. Because the farming is mainly pastoral, Fowler feels that there is a better chance of finding earthworks and occupation-sites of all periods, than in an area with the main emphasis on arable farming. For several reasons this project seems more like truly total archaeology than the Wiltshire one. Firstly, the existing cultural landscape is the starting point – the pattern which has continuously evolved since at least Anglo-Saxon times. Secondly, the unit of study is not, as before, a small natural zone like a block of downland, but the parish which is the basic economic, social and ecclesiastical unit of medieval and modern life. The main purpose will therefore be to study the evolution of the existing pattern of settlement and farming, with as many fragments of earlier patterns as can be found by exhaustive field-work. Thirdly, it is encouraging to learn that a local archivist is involved in the project, and that all available documentary evidence will be co-ordinated with the physical.

The second outstanding campaign of localized field-survey is being carried out by Professor Barry Cunliffe in an area of 20 square miles around the village of Chalton in east Hampshire.[13] It consists of one complete parish and parts of others, and is a strip across the dip-slope of the downs and the valleys to the south. Among Cunliffe's reasons for adopting this approach were the desire to study a piece of landscape fully, to cut across period boundaries, and to avoid 'the stranglehold of individual sites'. Intensive exploration on the ground coupled with the use of air-photographs has resulted in the discovery of many sites dating from prehistoric to medieval times. Earthworks and surface scatters of material have been systematically recorded, and a few sites have already been excavated.

Distribution maps of sites and finds discovered in the Chalton survey forcibly illustrate how thin and inadequate our normal patterns are: within the 20 square miles concerned, the concentration is much greater than outside, and is detailed and full enough to show striking relationships with the variations of geography and geology.[14] For example, while Mesolithic flints have been found *around* the edges of patches of clay-with-flints, remains of Neolithic axe-factories – clearly exploiting the natural nodules of flint – have been found actually *on* these patches of heavier land. Something approaching the full settlement pattern of the area in Roman times has been ascertained, with the finding of one villa, two villages and several farms, with remains of a complicated pattern of fields and linear boundaries Perhaps most impressive of all is the way in which the present settlement pattern evolved in Anglo-Saxon times. An extensive village on a hill-top, which yielded pottery of the 5th to 8th centuries, seems to have been superseded from the 9th century onwards by the present pattern of lowland villages. Of course with all these patterns, the blank areas are as significant as those where sites and finds occur. Firstly, they remind us of the element of choice in human affairs; there are always both positive and negative reasons why some sites were preferred to others. Secondly, they may well represent those areas which have been so intensively used (for instance, medieval common-fields) that evidence from earlier periods has been destroyed.

Most of the evidence discovered in this survey took the form of dead or fossil features belonging to medieval and earlier periods. However, Cunliffe was able to show how some of the old patterns have influenced life in modern times. For example, when an area of parkland was re-converted to agriculture in the 19th century, the new arable fields respected the ancient 'Celtic' lynchets and formed an almost identical pattern.

When documents are also worked into this study, as is Cunliffe's intention, the result will undoubtedly be the most detailed history of any piece of the English landscape from Mesolithic to modern times.

The work of both Fowler and Cunliffe has not only contributed to the history of the small areas they were concerned with, but has had considerable repercussions outside. For example the 13th-century long house at Raddun in Fyfield is now a type-site, and the grass-tempered pottery of the 5th to 8th centuries found by Cunliffe is now being recognized elsewhere. Highly localized archaeology therefore produces evidence which may be significant in much wider contexts, and confirms or reformulates many existing judgements and generalizations.[15]

On a slightly wider scale, we also have the example of some remarkable fieldwork done in East Anglia by Peter Wade-Martins.[16] In a dozen or so parishes in west Norfolk, he has intensively studied the evolution of the settlement-pattern, largely by surface scatters of pottery in ploughed land. This has cleverly made a virtue out of the traditional disadvantage of East Anglian archaeology: the paucity of earthworks as a result of intensive ploughing. The sites of several Middle and Late Saxon villages have been identified, usually in the vicinity of the church and often well away from the present village. This suggests that the phenomenon of the isolated church in East Anglia is connected, not with medieval plague and economic recession, but with largely unknown social and economic changes in Anglo-Saxon times. Wade-Martins was also able to show dramatic shifts or expansion of settlement to the edges of greens and commons in the 12th-14th centuries.

Localized work of this kind, covering the major part of a single hundred, is not in the fullest sense total archaeology: as Wade-Martins admits, the evidence for settlement at different periods was looked for only where there was some present-day link with the past (an isolated church, well-established roads, greens, moats, etc.). No parish was searched in its entirety, and therefore the degree of dispersed settlement in Anglo-Saxon and medieval times may be underestimated. Furthermore, apart from some excellent estate, enclosure and tithe maps, very few documents were used in this study.

Other deliberately localized pieces of research are being done; they are generally described as historical geography or topographical history. The main distinguishing features are a concentration on the evolution of the present landscape (usually a single parish or town), and the extensive use of written documents. The physical evidence used is mainly above-ground, such as the pattern of hedges, fields, commons, woods, roads, town-streets, defences, buildings and boundaries. In general this approach has been developed by people trained in geography or economic history. Thus the archaeology of the landscape has been cut into two distinct halves, the earlier periods studied by archaeologists and the later periods by geographers, economic historians and others. With the development of industrial and urban archaeology, this absurd dichotomy is now being broken down, but it still exists – above all in the study of rural areas.

Perhaps the study which has so far come nearest to total archaeology is C. C. Taylor's work on the single parish of Whiteparish in Wiltshire. Taylor is a geographer by training, and an archaeologist by profession. His approach is distinguished by a willingness to use all kinds of physical evidence, and to relate them to documents. In his own words 'this work has involved the study of many of the usual national and local records pertaining to the parish and it has been accompanied by a detailed examination on the ground. Every building and almost every field has been visited over a period of three years. Only in this way can the problems that faced the people of the parish be appreciated and understood.' Mention is made of such varied physical evidence as earthworks, scatters of pottery, buildings, fields, commons and boundaries. The published report is unfortunately a tantalizingly brief summary, which does no more than outline the settlement history of the parish over the last 1,500 years, and the way in which the fields steadily encroached on the natural wilderness. Nevertheless this study is important because of the *variety* of physical evidence used for a *limited* area: in this sense Taylor has come nearer the goal than have the other writers mentioned in this chapter. In his more recent book on the Dorset landscape, Taylor has again shown the same breadth of approach: using charters and other documents, place-names, boundaries, buried and surface archaeology, he makes by far the most convincing case yet published for continuity of settlement from Roman to medieval times.[17]

This appeal for total or local archaeology is a plea, not so much for a new specialization, as for the wider application of existing archaeological principles. One would like to see the archaeological contribution to the study of the landscape greatly strengthened, so that it balances the specifically historical and geographical contributions. A wide archaeological approach is necessary in order to weld together the great variety of physical evidence derived from excavation, field-survey, air-photographs and maps. Archaeologists are best fitted for this task of co-ordination, because by definition they specialize in physical evidence for broadly historical purposes – which is of course not true of historians, geographers, economists, architects, engineers and other groups who also study the cultural and natural landscape. It is much to the discredit of archaeologists that obvious landscape features like deserted villages were first studied and published by economic historians such as Hoskins and Beresford, and that industrial archaeology was really founded by engineers and architects.

Epilogue

If only historians of all kinds (including archaeologists) would reflect more on the critical philosophy and methodology of their subject, they would be better able to convince both educationists and the general public of the contemporary value of their craft. History explains the character and development of the contemporary world; it is the fragmentary record of human experience and wisdom; above all, it is a series of methods for distilling truth in the complicated web of human affairs. Historians no longer pretend to be able to foretell the future, but their role in explaining the present and in insisting on the sanctity of evidence should give them a burning mission to fulfil in the contemporary world.

An historian who professes to be uninterested in the present is probably a bad historian. Only when one is fascinated by the present, the way in which the carpet of history inexorably unfolds, by the unpredictability of the future, the way men influence events and events influence men, can one have the necessary imagination to see the men and women of the past trapped in the same process. Although there are other motives involved, in the last resort we study history because we are baffled and fascinated by the complexities of the present. This does not mean that we should not study the past as objectively as possible, that we should judge the past by present standards, or that we should only seek to explain and measure the present. The study of the past has values and rewards of its own, but basically because, being trapped in the present, and our own particular present at that, we are anxious to know how others have coped with the challenges of life. Not only is the present the starting-point of any historical research because the raw material (whether documents or archaeological artifacts) must be things which survive *now*, but it is also the stimulus which should drive us into the past, and give us the desire to undertake the considerable discipline involved.

Annotations

CHAPTER 1 (pp. 9–21)

1 C. F. C. Hawkes, *Proceedings Prehistoric Society*, XVII (1951), pp. 1-15. In his presidential address, Hawkes also proposed the use of the following terms: ante-historic, tele-historic, para-historic and pene-historic.

2 Glyn Daniel, *The Origins and Growth of Archaeology,* (1967), pp. 24-5.

3 Glyn Daniel, *The Idea of Prehistory*, (1962), p. 123.

4 Stuart Piggott, *Approach to Archaeology*, (1966), Pelican, p. 13. R. J. C. Atkinson, *Archaeology, History and Science*, (1960), p. 21.

5 R. G. Collingwood, *The Idea of History*, (1946), p. 277.

6 E. Estyn Evans, *Irish Folk Ways* (1957), p. xiii.

7 V. Gordon Childe, *Piecing Together the Past*, (1956), p. 1.

8 Stuart Piggott, *op. cit.*, p. 29.

CHAPTER 2 (pp. 22–49)

1 C. Hawkes, 'Archaeological theory and method: some suggestions from the Old World', *American Anthropologist*, 56, p. 156. A rather unsuitable term which suggests liberation rather than limitation!

2 L. Biek in Brothwell and Higgs (eds), *Science in Archaeology* (1969), p. 567.

3 J. M. Coles, *Studies in Ancient Europe* (1968), pp. 23-4.

4 Hayman Rooke, 'Some account of the Brimham Rocks in Yorkshire', *Archaeologia*, VIII, pp. 209-17.

5 See F. H. Thompson, *Antiquaries Journal*, L (1970), p. 93 for summary and further references.

6 A. Raistrick and P. F. Holmes, 'Archaeology of Malham Moor', *Field Studies*, Vol. 1, No. 4 (1962), pp. 73-100.

7 See for example F. T. Wainwright, *Archaeology and place-names and history*, (1962), p. 8.

8 See Adolf Rieth, *Archaeological fakes* (1967, English translation), bibliography on p. 181.

9 In fact we have a good historical example of precisely this kind of

speculation. In his *Antiquities of Warwickshire* (1656), p. 778 William Dugdale makes one of the earliest-recorded recognitions in Britain of a prehistoric implement; he reasoned that a small axe was man-made, that it had been deliberately shaped and ground, that one end 'was shaped much like the edge of a Pole-Axe', that it was found in an area more than 40 miles from the nearest source of flint, that it had probably been hafted, and that it was a weapon made by people ignorant of metals. These are brilliant examples at an early date of the historical interpretation of archaeological evidence.

10 K. C. Chang, *Rethinking archaeology* (1967), p. 109.

11 See F. S. Wallis 'Petrological examination' in *The Scientist and Archaeology* (ed. Edward Pyddoke, 1963), pp. 80-100; F. W. Shotton, 'Petrological examination' in *Science in Archaeology* (ed. Brothwell and Higgs, 1969) pp. 571-7. Essentially similar work has been carried out on the analysis of Greek marbles, in order to relate broken sculptural fragments and to identify the source of the rock. See N. Herz and W. K. Pritchett, 'Marble in Attic epigraphy', *American Journal of Anthropology*, Vol. 57, pp. 71-83.

12 Royal Commission on Historical Monuments, 'Wareham West Walls', *Medieval Archaeology*, Vol. 3 (1959), pp. 120-38.

13 *Ibid.*, pp. 126 and 130: 'In view of the subsequent history of the defences, it seems reasonable to regard the rim (No. 15), of approximately Norman age, as an intrusion . . . This sherd . . . although found in the lower part of the primary rampart, was not in a position that would preclude the possibility of subsequent intrusion through natural or other agencies'.

14 V. Gordon Childe, *Piecing together the past* (1956), p. 124.

15 It happened for instance in the history of the pre-Roman coinage of Gaul and Britain. In 1849 Sir John Evans showed that these coins were derived from the *stater* of Philip II of Macedonia and that the originally naturalistic design was allowed to disintegrate into a pattern of meaningless shapes. (*Numismatic Chronicle*, Vol. XII (1850), pp. 127-37.).

16 R. J. C. Atkinson, *Archaeology, history and science* (1965), p. 17.

17 See for example, D. A. Roe, 'British Lower and Middle Palaeolithic hand-axe groups', *Proceedings of Prehistoric Soc. N. S. XXXIV* (1968), pp. 1-82. For a more recent example of such work, see D. L. Clarke, *Beaker pottery of Great Britain and Ireland* (1970), 2 vols.

18 See Frederick E. Zeuner, *Dating the Past* (1958, 4th edition); Broth-well and Higgs (eds.), *Science in Archaeology* (1969, 2nd edition) Section 1.

19 C. B. M. McBurney in Brothwell and Higgs (eds.), *op. cit.* (1963 ed.), pp. 21-2.

20 'The radio-carbon revolution', *Current Archaeology*, No. 18 (Jan. 1970), pp. 180-4. For fuller information see *The impact of the natural science on archaeology* (1970), pp. 1-45.

21 V. G. Childe, *The Danube in prehistory* (1929), Preface p. vi.

22 Bray and Trump, *A dictionary of archaeology* (1970), p. 68.

23 The possibility of exploratory and punitive expeditions to such areas should not be forgotten: these could leave monumental traces.

24 See W. Y. Adams, 'Invasion, diffusion, evolution', *Antiquity*, XLII (1968), p. 194.

25 Stuart Piggott, *Approach to archaeology* (1966 Pelican), p. 99.

26 *ex. inf.* E. S. Higgs.

27 Binford and Binford (eds.), *New perspectives in archaeology* (1968).

28 C. Hawkes, *American Anthropologist*, 56, pp. 155-68. This develops the ideas of Gordon Childe in his *Social Evolution* (1951).

29 See for example James N. Hill, 'Broken K. Pueblo: patterns of forms and function' in Binford and Binford (eds.), *op. cit.* (1968), pp. 103-42.

30 Sir John Clapham, *A concise history of Britain* (1949), Introduction.

31 See J. C. Harriss, 'Explanation in prehistory', *Proceedings Prehistoric Soc.* XXXVII (1971), pp. 38-55; Council for British Archaeology, *Handbook of scientific aids and evidence for archaeologists* (1970).

32 J. M. Coles in Brothwell and Higgs (eds.), *op. cit.*, (1963 ed.) p. 93.

33 C. McBurney, *The Haua Fteah (Cyrenaica) and the Stone Age of the S. E. Mediterranean* (1967).

34 David L. Clarke, *Analytical archaeology* (1968).

35 Brothwell and Higgs (eds.), *op. cit.*, (1963 ed.), p. 15.

36 Glyn Daniel, *The origins and growth of archaeology* (1967), Preface.

37 B. G. Trigger, 'Aims in prehistoric archaeology', *Antiquity*, XLIV (1970), p. 26.

38 Jacquetta Hawkes, 'The proper study of mankind', *Antiquity*, XLII (1968), p. 258.

39 R. J. C. Atkinson, *Archaeology, history and science* (1960), p. 30.

CHAPTER 3 (pp. 50–74)

1 In many ways the best manual is still C. V. Langlois and C. Seignobos, *Introduction to the study of history* (1898). A useful recent survey of historiography is Arthur Marwick, *The nature of history* (1970).

2 See E. L. C. Mullins, *Texts and calendars, an analytical guide to serial publications* (1958).

3 G. R. Elton, *The practice of history* (1967), pp. 68-70.

4 See Glyn Daniel, *The origins and growth of archaeology* (1967), pp. 205-18.

5 John Chadwick, *The decipherment of Linear B* (1958).

6 E.g. L. C. Hector, *The handwriting of English documents* (1958);

C. T. Martin, *The record interpreter* (2nd edition 1910); C. Johnson and H. Jenkinson, *English court hand 1066-1500* (1915).

7 G. Kitson Clark, *The critical historian* (1967), pp. 87-92 for a brief history of shorthand, which has its origins in the Tironian system of classical times.

8 David Diringer, *Writing,* (1962), pp. 154-5.

9 Kathleen Major, 'The teaching and study of Diplomatic in England', *Archives*, Vol. VIII (April, 1968), pp. 114-18.

10 C. G. Grump, 'What became of Robert Rag?' in *Essays presented to T. F. Tout* (1925), pp. 335-47.

11 See L. C. Hector, *Palaeography and forgery* (1959), pp. 11-12, also Plate III. Strictly the document was a 'foot of fine', the bottom piece of a tripartite indenture.

12 See F. W. Hall, *Companion to classical texts* (1913); A. C. Clark, *The descent of manuscripts* (1918).

13 Hubert Hall, *A formula book of English official historical documents* Part I (1908), Part II (1909); Thomas Madox, *Formulare Anglicanum* (1702).

14 E.g. Powicke and Fryde (eds.), *Handbook of British Chronology* (1961); C. R. Cheney, *Handbook of Dates for students of English history* (1961).

15 Langlois and Seignobos *op. cit.,* especially Book II, Chapter VII.

16 It almost goes without saying that these sources were not necessarily called chronicles by their authors, but may be masquerading under such titles as Sagas, Lives, Annals, Histories, etc. See J. Taylor, *The use of medieval chronicles* (1965).

17 Matthew Paris, *Chronica majora*, ed. H. R. Luard, 7 vols. (Rolls Series, 1872-84).

18 Joseph Addison (1672-1719) expressed the difference between a chronicle and record thus: 'it is much safer to quote a medal than an author for in this case you do not appeal to Suetonius or to Lamprisius, but to the Emperor himself or to the whole body of a Roman Senate.' (Quoted in *Journal Warburg Inst.,* 12-13 (1949-50), p. 299.)

19 Kitson Clark, *The critical historian* (1967), particularly Ch. 9.

20 E. H. Dance, *History the betrayer* (1960), pp. 9-10.

21 E. H. Carr, *What is history?* (1964, Pelican), p. 10.

22 G. J. Renier, *History, its purpose and method* (1950), p. 95.

23 For example of the scholarly treatment of documentary forms and administrative machinery see C. R. Cheney, *English bishops' chanceries 1100-1250* (1950); Geoffrey Barraclough, *Public notaries and the Papal Curia* (1934).

24 For an interesting discussion of 'cliometrics' or 'econometrics', see Peter Mathias, 'Economic history—direct and oblique' in Martin

Ballard (ed.), *New movements in the study and teaching of history* (1971).

25 W. G. Hoskins, *Local history in England* (1959), p. 20.

26 R. W. Fogel, *Railroads and American economic growth: essays in econometric history* (1965).

CHAPTER 4 (pp. 75–108)

1 R. E. M. Wheeler, *Archaeology from the earth* (1954), pp. 2-3.

2 R. E. M. Wheeler, *Antiquity* XLII (1968), p. 295.

3 Dom David Knowles, *The historian and character* (1964), p. 254.

4 D. P. Dymond, *Archaeology for the historian* (1967, Hist. Assoc.), p. 9.

5. E. H. Carr, *What is History?* (1961, Penguin) p. 50.

6 R. J. C. Atkinson, *Archaeology, history and science* (1960), p. 8.

7 T. S. Ashton, *An economic history of England: the 18th century* (1955), p. 17.

8 R. E. M. Wheeler, *Maiden Castle, Dorset* (1943).

9 For the siege of Masada, see Josephus, *The Jewish War,* Book VII 275-406. Other examples of 'events' caught in the archaeological record are mentioned in R. F. Heizer (ed.), *The archaeologist at work* (1959), pp. 1-24.

10 R. J. C. Atkinson, *Archaeology, history and science* (1960), p. 20.

11 G. Kitson Clark, *The critical historian* (1967), p. 1.

12 Christopher and Jacquetta Hawkes, *Prehistoric Britain* (1949), Foreword.

13 Archivists who wrestle with the problem of contemporary records, mainly from local and national government, have to assume the frightening responsibility of systematically discarding many documents – simply because there is not enough room to keep everything. See *Report of Committee on Departmental Records* (1954) Command 9163; *Journal Soc. Archivists* (Oct. 1962; Oct. 1966; Oct. 1968).

14 G. R. Elton, *England 1200-1640* (1969), p. 234.

15 Barlow and Harrison, *History at the universities* (1966, Historical Association); Harold Perkin (ed.) *History: an introduction for the intending student* (1970).

16 Prof. A. Marwick of the Open University has written in his *Nature of History* (1970), p. 9: 'I would myself go so far as to argue that the survey courses which at present form the usual introduction to history at university and college level ought to be scrapped in favour of courses which treat of the nature and purposes of history.' For a recent discussion of these issues, see *History*, LIII (Oct. 1968) and LIV (Feb. 1969).

17 K. C. Chang, *Rethinking archaeology* (1967), p. 137 recommends the idea of 'Archaeological Information Storage Centers' around the

world 'where archaeological data are processed, computerized, and stored'.

18 Jacquetta Hawkes, *Antiquity*, XLII (1968), p. 256.

19 R. J. C. Atkinson, *op. cit.* (1960), p. 11.

20 Stuart Piggott, *Approach to archaeology* (1966, Pelican), p. 103.

21 See John Alexander, *The directing of archaeological excavations* (1970).

22 For an interesting discussion of the possibilities of doing more co-operative work in history, see V. H. T. Skipp, 'The place of team-work in local history' in Finberg and Skipp, *Local history, objective and pursuit* (1967), pp. 87-102.

23 Council for British Archaeology, *2nd memo. on historic towns* (July 1965).

24 W. G. Hoskins, *English local history, the past and the future* (1966), p. 5.

25 H. P. R. Finberg, *Local history in the university* (1964), p. 5.

26 R. Allen Brown, 'An historian's approach to the origins of the castle in England', *Archaeological Journal,* CXXVI (1969), p. 132.

27 D. P. Agrawal, 'Archaeology and the Luddites', *Antiquity,* XLIV (1970), p. 115.

28 R. Allen Brown, *Archaeological Journal,* CXXVI (1969), pp. 132 ff. On pp. 146 ff. B. Davison, archaeologist, replies.

29 In Britain, the Ancient Monuments Inspectorate are now com-missioning historical research in conjunction with the excavation of medieval sites. This is obviously an excellent development. On the other hand, official guides to monuments frequently consist of two quite unrelated sections – an archaeological analysis by one writer, and an historical account by another.

30 G. R. Elton, *The practice of history* (1967), p. 71.

31 One person who pondered the problems of co-ordination was the late Frederick Wainwright. In his *Archaeology and place-names and history* (1962), which was sub-titled *An essay on problems of co-ordination*, he put forward many challenging ideas, worked out in the relatively narrow context of the Anglo-Saxon period but of general application.

32 H. Wharton, *Anglia Sacra,* I, pp. 591-688. The chronicle is des-cribed as Chronicon Abbatum et Episcoporum Eliensium by E. O. Blake, *Liber Eliensis,* Camden Soc., Vol. XCII (1962), p. xxvi.

33 E. R. Chapman, *Sacrist Rolls of Ely*, (1907), 2 vols.

34 G. G. Coulton, *Social life in Britain from the Conquest to the Re-formation* (1919), p. 480.

35 Nikolaus Pevsner, *The buildings of England, Cambridgeshire* (1954), p. 281; L. F. Salzman, *Building in England down to 1540* (1952), pp.

6-7, 390.

36 Maurice Beresford in his *History on the ground* (1957, revised 1971) provides many good examples of this kind of identification.

37 J. M. Dodgson, *Medieval Archaeology*, X (1966), p. 1.

38 F. T. Wainwright, *op. cit* (1962) p. 111.

CHAPTER 5 (pp. 109–132)
1 See J. E. Sandys, *A short history of classical scholarship* (1915).

2 See Albin Lasky, *A history of Greek literature* (1966).

3 J. Adam, *Republic of Plato* (1902, 2nd ed. 1963).

4 J. G. C. Anderson, *Tacitus: de origine et situ Germanorum* (1938), pp. lxii-lxiv.

5 Aristophanes, *The Clouds,* ed. K. J. Dover (1968), p. xcix.

6 See F. W. Hall, *Companion to classical texts* (1913).

7 See M. Hadas, *Ancilla to classical reading* (1954).

8 *The letters of the Younger Pliny* (1963, Penguin), Book 6, pp. 171-2. Translation by Betty Radice.

9 Sir Ian Richmond, *Hod Hill,* Vol. 2 (1969), p. 33.

10 H. E. Salter, *Oxford charters* (1929), p. 100.

11 T. F. Tout, *Collected papers* Vol. III, p. 117. Tout was by no means the first to expose this fraud. In 1695 Henry Wharton pointed out many inconsistencies in his *History of the Bishops and Deans of London and St Asaph.*

12 *Guide to seals in PRO* (1954), p. 1. This definition is acceptable in the context of medieval history, but it should not be forgotten that seals have been in common use since at least 3500 BC, and can even antedate writing. See Bray and Trump, *A dictionary of archaeology* (1970), p. 206.

13 *Guide to seals in PRO* (1954), pp. 3-4.

14 C. N. L. Brooke, *Medieval miscellany,* Pipe Roll Soc. (1960), pp. 45-63.

15 See C. Boutell, *Handbook of English Heraldry* (1958 ed.); W. H. St J. Hope, *Grammar of English Heraldry* (revd. A. R. Wagner, 1953).

16 'Tricking' is the delineation of armorial bearings in black and white, often using various kinds of hatching as conventions for colours.

17 J. H. Round, *Geoffrey de Mandeville* (1892), pp. 388-96, Table on p. 392.

18 Sir Harris Nicolas, *The Roll of Arms known as the Roll of King Henry III* (Glover's), n.d.

19 Charles Boutell, *English heraldry* (1875), p. 23.

20 H. M. Colvin, 'Architectural history and its records', *Archives,* Vol. II, p. 300.

21 I am indebted to Dr E. A. Gee for pointing out the significance

of Parker's work. For other examples of architectural and documentary co-ordination, see L. F. Salzman, *Building in England down to 1540* (1952), especially appendices A, B, and C, pp. 355-594.

22 R. Willis, *Architectural history of Winchester cathedral* (1846); with J. W. Clark, *Architectural history of the University of Cambridge* (1886).

23 H. M. and J. Taylor, *Anglo-Saxon architecture* (1965), Vol. 1, p. 1.

24 John H. Fisher, *John Gower* (1965), Chapter 2.

25 J. S. Ackerman, *Art and archaeology* (with R. Carpenter, 1963) p. 134.

26 D. Talbot Rice, 'The history of art' in H. P. R. Finberg (ed.), *Approaches to History* (1962), p. 158.

27 F. Wormald, 'The Wilton Diptych', *Journal Warburg Institute,* 17 (1954), p. 191.

28 M. V. Clarke, *Fourteenth century studies* (1937), pp. 272-92.

29 M. Galway, *Archaeological Journal,* Vol. 107 (1950), pp. 9-14.

30 V. H. Galbraith, *An introduction to the study of history* (1964), p. 71.

31 Margaret Rickert, *Painting in Britain: the Middle Ages* (1954), pp. 157-60.

32 Thomas Bodkin, *The Wilton Diptych in the National Gallery, London* (Gallery Books, n.d.), pp. 3 and 4; Joan Evans, *English Art 1307-1461* (1949) p. 102.

CHAPTER 6 (pp. 133–158)

1 A. Hadrian Allcroft, *Earthwork of England* (1908), Ch. XVI, pp. 550-3.

2 Lincoln Record Society, *The Lincolnshire Domesday and the Lindsey Survey* (1924), appendices I and III.

3 *Transactions of the Leicestershire Archaeological Society,* XXII (1944-5), pp. 241-64.

4 J. H. Clapham, *Concise economic history of Great Britain* (1949), p. 197.

5 Deserted Medieval Village Research Group, 67 Gloucester Crescent, London, N. W. 1. See M. Beresford and J. G. Hurst, *Deserted Medieval Villages* (1971). There is a useful summary of the whole subject in K. J. Allison, *Deserted villages* (1970).

6 DMVRG *Annual reports* (from 1954); *Medieval archaeology* (from 1957).

7 DMVRG *Annual report*, particularly 1963 and subsequently. P.S. The post-holes of an even earlier church have now been found (DMVRG Report No. 19, 1971).

8 Maurice Beresford, *The lost villages of England* (1965, 5th impression), pp. 292-3.

9 Abuttals are written descriptions of individual properties (whether buildings or plots of land) by reference to the properties or landscape features which bound or abut them, often on all four sides. The details given can include the names of present and former occupiers, field and tenement names, acreages, tenure and land-use.

10 Margaret Spufford, *A Cambridgeshire community, Chippenham from settlement to enclosure* (1965).

11 *Urban history newsletter* (from 1962).

12 H. J. Dyos, *Victorian suburb, a study of the growth of Camberwell* (1961).

13 G. H. Martin, 'The town as palimpsest', *The study of urban history*, ed. H. J. Dyos (1968), p. 155.

14 H. E. Salter, *Medieval Oxford* (1936); *Map of Medieval Oxford* (1934). His *Survey of Oxford* is now being edited by W. A. Pantin, Vol. I (1960), Vol. II (1968).

15 W. Urry, *Canterbury under the Angevin Kings* (1967).

16 R. N. Quirk, *Archaeological Journal*, CXIV (1957), pp. 66-8; Martin Biddle and R. N. Quirk, *Archaeological Journal*, CXIX (1962), pp. 173-82. For a summary of these excavations see Martin Biddle, *The Old Minister, excavations near Winchester cathedral 1961-69* (1970).

17 R. N. Quirk, *Archaeological Journal*, CXIV (1957), p. 44.

18 M. Biddle, *Antiquaries Journal* (1967), pp. 259-60.

19 'Winchester, the Brooks', *Current Archaeology*, No. 20 (May 1970). pp. 250-55.

20 Martin Biddle, 'Archaeology and the history of towns', *Antiquity*, XLII (1968), p. 109.

21 For a useful introduction, see T. H. Hollingsworth, *Historical Demography* (1969).

22 *Local population studies magazine and newsletter* (from 1968, twice yearly).

23 For places and periods for which no documentation exists, see W. W. Howells, 'Estimating population numbers through archaeological and skeletal remains' in Heizer and Cook, *The application of quantitative methods in archaeology* (1960), pp. 158 ff.

24 The VAG also produces a bulletin, and since 1970 a journal called *Vernacular architecture*.

25 W. G. Hoskins, *Fieldwork in local history* (1967), p. 94. See also H. M. Colvin, *A guide to the sources of English architectural history* (1967); M. W. Barley, *The English farmhouse and cottage* (1961).

26 M. W. Barley, A. Rogers and P. Strange, 'The medieval parsonage house, Coningsby, Lincolnshire', *Antiquaries Journal*, XLIX (1969), p. 346. An excellent example of co-ordination.

27 *Vernacular Architecture*, 2 (1971), p. 10.

28 Collections of title-deeds which go with the possession of specific named properties provide a fascinating example of the association of things and words.

29 A. G. Matthews, *Calamy revised* (1934), p. 424.

30 Publication forthcoming, D. P. Dymond and Mrs S. Colman.

31 M. Rix in *Amateur Historian*, Vol. 2, No. 8 (Oct-Nov 1955). See also Kenneth Hudson, *Industrial archaeology* (1963) and Michael Rix, *Industrial archaeology* (1967); R. A. Buchanan, *Industrial archaeology in Britain* (1972); all three have bibliographies.

32 *Journal of industrial archaeology* (from 1964). A good example of excavation in this field is at Gawber glass-house, Yorks in *Post-medieval archaeology*, Vol. 4 (1970), pp. 92-140.

33 R. F. Heizer, *The archaeologist at work* (1959), p. 210.

34 See O. Rackham (ed.) *Hayley Wood, Cambridgeshire* (forthcoming), Cambs. and Isle of Ely Naturalists' Trust.

35 See W. G. Hoskins, *Field work in local history* (1967), Chapter 8; M. D. Hooper, 'Dating hedges', *Area*, Vol. 4 (1970), pp. 63-5; M. D. Hooper, W. G. Hoskins *et al., Hedges and Local History* (1971) N.C.S.S.

CHAPTER 7 (pp. 159–175)

1 W. G. Hoskins, *Local History in England* (1959), p. 15.

2 The more detailed approach of the total archaeologist, though still to some extent selective, also means that relatively minor and late features are surveyed which would normally be overlooked. Such objects as clearance-mounds, sheep-pens, windmill-steadings, charcoal-burners' huts and shielings are as much the product of human industry as anything listed above, and the fact that they are commonly mis-interpreted shows that they too deserve a record and explanation. See Ramm, McDowell and Mercer, *Shielings and bastles* (1970); J. R. Mortimer, *40 years researches in ... burial mounds of E. Yorkshire* (n.d.) pp. 388-96 for misinterpretation of windmill-steadings.

3 E. S. Higgs, in *The Listener*, Vol. 77 (1967), pp. 425-7.

4 *Current Archaeology*, No. 16 (Sept. 1969), p. 124.

5 The Society for Historical Archaeology was founded in America in 1967. See I. Noël Hume, *Historical Archaeology*, (1969).

6 For the two sides of this controversy, see *14th Annual Report, 1967* of the Ancient Monuments Boards (1968) for 'purist' advice to the Minister of Public Building and Works; *16th Annual Report, 1968* of the Historic Buildings Council (1969) for 'evolutionary' advice to the Minister of Housing and Local Government! This sorry tale of bureaucrative delay and municipal parsimony is still unresolved (February, 1972).

7 This account is based on a lecture given by Professor Cunliffe to

the Society of Antiquaries, London, in Feb. 1970.

8 L. Butler has carried out a similar project at Faxton, Northants. The 17th-century Rectory Farm was demolished in 1959, and subsequent excavation proved that the site had been occupied from the 12th to 15th centuries, but then abandoned. See *Current Archaeology*, No. 16 (Sept. 1969), pp. 145-6. See also Survey of London, Vol. XXVIII, *The parish of Hackney, Part 1: Brooke House* (1960).

9 *Current Archaeology*, No. 16 (Sept. 1969), p. 129.

10 William Camden, *Britannia* (translated Philemon Holland, 1610), author's preface.

11 Arthur Raistrick, *Pennine Walls* (1961); *The Making of the English Landscape, West Riding* (1970).

12 Peter Fowler, 'Fyfield Down 1959-68', *Current Archaeology*, No. 16 (Sept. 1969), pp. 124-29. For more detailed reports, see *Wiltshire Archaeological Magazine*, 57 (1960) onwards.

13 Lecture given to the Society of Antiquaries, London, Feb. 1970.

14 See V. Gordon Childe, *The Danube in Prehistory* (1929), p. ix: what distribution maps so often indicate 'is not a real distribution, but the distinction between well-studied and virtually unexplored regions'.

15 The work of A. Steensberg at Borup Ris, Denmark is surely the most painstaking attempt ever made at area-survey: by planning earthworks on a large scale, by probing at frequent intervals (at least 100 times in each 5 metre square), and by selective excavation, he aims to reconstruct the farming history of an area of 200 hectares (*c.* 4,900 acres). Frankly, it remains to be seen whether the historical results are commensurate with the fantastic labour involved. Ed. A. Steensberg, *Atlas over Borups Agre 1000-1200 e. Kr.* (1968).

16 P. Wade-Martins, *The development of the landscape and human settlement in West Norfolk . . . 350-1650 AD*, Leicester Univ. Ph. D. thesis (1971).

17 C. C. Taylor, 'Whiteparish', *Wiltshire Archaeological Magazine*, Vol. 62 (1967), pp. 79-102; *Making of the English Landscape, Dorset* (1970).

Bibliography

Atkinson, R. J. C. *Archaeology, history and science* Cardiff 1965.
Beresford, Maurice *History on the ground* London 1957.
Bray, Warwick and Trump, David *A dictionary of archaeology* Harmondsworth 1970.
Brothwell, Don and Higgs, Eric (eds.), *Science in archaeology* (2nd ed.), London 1969.
Chang, K. C. *Rethinking archaeology* New York 1967.
Childe, V. Gordon *Piecing together the past* London 1956.
Clarke, David L. *Analytical archaeology* London 1968.
Daniel, Glyn *The idea of prehistory* London 1962.
—*The origins and growth of archaeology* Harmondsworth 1967.
Finberg, H. P. R. (ed.) *Approaches to history* London 1962.
Fowler, P. J. (ed.) *Archaeology and the landscape* London 1972.
Hoskins, W. G. *Fieldwork in local history* London 1967.
Kitson Clark, G. *The critical historian* London 1967.
Marwick, Arthur *The nature of history* London 1970.
Langlois, C. V. and Seignobos, C. *Introduction to the study of history* London 1898.
Rogers, Alan *This was their world: approaches to local history* London 1972.
Salzman, L. F. *Building in England* Oxford 1952.
Wainwright, F. T. *Archaeology and place-names and history* London 1962.

Index